# Power Persuasion

## Using Hypnotic Influence in Life, Love and Business

by
### David R. Barron
and
### Danek S. Kaus

Robert D. Reed Publishers • Bandon, OR

Robert D. Reed Publishers
P.O. Box 1992
Bandon, OR 97411
Phone: 541-347-9882 • Fax: -9883
E-mail: 4bobreed@msn.com
web site: www.rdrpublishers.com


Typesetter: **Barbara Kruger**
Cover Designer: **Grant Prescott**
Editor: **Cleone Lyvonne**


ISBN 1-931741-52-2

Library of Congress Control Number 2005901199


Manufactured, typeset and printed in the United States of America

# Dedications

First, to my Mother, Shirley Barron, who fearlessly
introduced me to this life.
And especially to Linda, my sweetheart,
my best friend,
my business partner,
my biggest fan and
my inspiration
I hope to see you in the next life as well.

David


To my parents, Shirley and Daniel Kaus.
Thank you for all you have taught me.
Thank you for your encouragement.
And most of all
Thank you for always being there.

With love,

Danny

# Contents

# What This Book Can Do For You

What do you want out of life?

More money? Success in business? A beautiful home? A loving, supportive relationship? Recognition? A better job?

Almost everything we want to have or achieve requires the cooperation of other people. In order to make a sale, you have to get someone to sign the agreement and give you a check. To obtain a mortgage, you have to convince the loan officer you are a good risk.

If you want to go out with that interesting looking man or woman, which could lead to romance, you have to first convince that person you are someone worth investing at least one evening with.

If you want a raise, you must persuade your boss that you are worth the extra money.

Maybe you just want your kids to clean their rooms and turn down the stereo.

Power Persuasion will give you the tools to help make your dreams come true. It will teach you many of the most powerful persuasion techniques that have ever been created

Power Persuasion will show you how to influence people to see things your way, to say yes and feel good about it.

If you want to learn these secrets, read on.

---

**Almost everything you want
requires the cooperation of other people.**

# CHAPTER 1

# What Is Persuasion?

Persuasion is that seemingly magical ability to influence other people and to influence yourself to move in the direction that you most want.

Persuasion is the ability to know what someone else is thinking before they know they are thinking it.

Persuasion is the ability to change the world.

## THE MOST IMPORTANT PERSON
## YOU CAN EVER PERSUADE

Who is this person?

You are.

In order for your dreams to come true, you must first convince yourself that they are attainable and you must convince yourself to take action.

Take a few moments now to convince yourself that you really can become a powerful persuader.

Here's how:

Imagine a time in your future when you've practiced each one of the exercises and learned each one of the skills and know that you can instantly influence and persuade anyone on a very positive level. You can hear yourself say with great confidence those things which are most important and true for you and know that they are influencing the people with which you talk.

As you see this and as you hear those words and you feel that sense of control and power in your very actions, you will probably notice that there is a profound sense of feeling calm as well.

This calmness comes from knowing that you can do anything.

This is the power to persuade.

> **Persuasion is that seemingly magical ability to influence other people and yourself.**

## A WORD OF WARNING

The techniques you are about to learn are extremely powerful.

They are based on a profound understanding of how the mind works. The language patterns you will learn have powerful hypnotic effects that can reach someone's unconscious mind and influence it in dramatic ways.

Is this manipulation?

You betcha.

Is it moral?

The meaning of the word manipulate is "To move with intent." If you pick up a pen you are manipulating the pen. Whenever you are persuading someone you are intentionally trying to move them in a specific direction.

Like any other power, manipulation is neither good nor bad. It is your intention that determines the ethics of what you are doing.

When Dan was a young boy, he was a fan of Davy Crockett. But he was not a fan of liver. The only reason he ate it was because his parents told him it was bear meat, something that his idol Davy surely ate in large quantities.

Was this manipulation on his parents' part?

Yes.

Was it moral?

Definitely.

Today's children face a much more serious threat than proper nutrition. On an almost daily basis they are exposed to the temptation to take illegal drugs.

Would it be moral for parents to use these techniques to keep their children off drugs? We believe so.

On the other hand, if you sell a client a $10,000 widget with bells and whistles you know he will never use, when you could have offered him a $6,000 one that would more than meet his needs, you have stepped over a line.

How you use Power Persuasion is ultimately up to you.

We strongly suggest that you use these tools in ways that benefit everyone involved.

DO NOT manipulate your friends, romantic partners and business associates for selfish purposes.

We encourage using Power Persuasion with integrity for two reasons.

First, because it is the right thing to do.

Second, because the things we do in life have a tendency to come back to us, if not now, then sometime when we least expect it. Whether this happens because of an all-seeing Deity, karma or the workings of our own subconscious minds, you will reap what you sow.

If you use these techniques in ways that are harmful, events and situations will eventually backfire on you. Trust can be broken and friendships lost. Opportunities will slip from your grasp. Doors will close forever.

We hope you will use what you learn in these pages with integrity. On the other hand, if you lack the basic moral fiber to treat people fairly, then at least adopt a healthy sense of self-preservation with regard to these techniques.

You have been warned.

## THE E WORD

Throughout this book, we are going to use what many people consider a dirty word—Exercise. We will also use another offensive word—Practice.

Each of the Power Persuasion techniques you are about to learn is followed by one or more exercises. In order to become truly skilled with these techniques and make them your own, you must do each of the exercises and practice the techniques.

More than once.

And more than a few times.

After all, you can't learn to drive a car by reading the DMV booklet. You have to get behind the wheel and actually practice driving.

Nor can you produce a beautiful painting by reading a book on technique. You have to put paint to canvas to develop your art.

The same is true with Power Persuasion. It is not enough to simply read about the techniques. You may think that's enough, but it's not.

Some of you may have encountered some of this material before and think you know it. Do the exercises anyway. If you don't, you will be the one who loses.

So do the exercises.

Practice the techniques to make them your own.

# CHAPTER 2

# Developing Competence

## A MICKEY MOUSE LESSON

Remember Mickey Mouse as the sorcerer's apprentice? Like any other apprenticeship, learning magic was preceded by performing a bunch of mundane chores such as sweeping the floor and carrying water.

One day Mickey watched his master perform a magical feat. Mickey was sure he finally knew how to do magic. So when his master was away, Mickey used magic to animate a broom to go out to the well and bring water into the house.

It worked perfectly. Until Mickey wanted the broom to stop. Try as he might, the lazy apprentice could not keep the broom from going out to the well. Soon the water began to overfill all the receptacles in the house. Mickey still could not get it to stop. Desperate, he chopped up the broom. Instead of ending the situation, he produced dozens of brooms, each of which brought more and more water into the house, filling it with so much water that Mickey was in danger of drowning. Only when the master returned were the brooms halted and Mickey saved.

Don't let that happen to you. If you attempt to use Power Persuasion techniques in important situations before you have mastered them, you will get in over your head.

Although you may not drown, the other person will think you are all wet.

Trust us, soggy people are seldom persuasive. And if you botch a technique at a critical time, there is no master to come clear up the mess you've made.

So do the exercises.

## Unconscious Competence

Unconscious?

Who wants to be unconscious?

You do.

Let us explain.

There are four levels of performance:

**Unconscious incompetence**—this is when you don't know how to do something and you don't realize that you don't know how. Using the driving analogy again, a young teenager who has never had driver training may think he knows how to drive the family car. So he steals the keys when his parents are asleep, cranks up the engine and drives the car into a tree. This is a real world example of unconscious incompetence.

**Conscious incompetence**—the kid realizes he needs to take driving lessons. Once his period of being grounded is over, he signs up for driver education.

**Conscious competence**—he's taken the lessons and passed his driving test. He has a license but he's not a skilled driver. He has to focus intently on everything he is doing. Oncoming cars whizzing by make him nervous. If the car has a manual transmission, he has to consciously think about where each gear position is while trying to press and release the clutch pedal at the right time, while keeping the car between the lines. Every now and then his timing is off and gears grind. But he can drive from point A to point B.

**Unconscious competence**—our hero has been driving for several months now. He chats to the girl sitting next to him while the stereo blasts. Oncoming traffic no longer intimidates him. As he approaches a stoplight he automatically downshifts without thinking about it. The stick shift glides into place as the conversation continues without interruption. He has driven for so many hours that he no longer has to think about the specifics of what his hands and feet are doing. The skill set is now part of his unconscious mind. This frees his conscious mind to focus on traffic. We hope.

We want you to become so adept at Power Persuasion that you no longer have to think about which techniques to employ when or to try to recall the specific phrasing that has proven to be so effective for a particular objection. When you have unconscious competence, you are able to focus on what the other person is saying and doing so that you can respond in the most appropriate and effective way.

This is why doing the exercises and practicing them is so important. When you have unconscious competence with Power Persuasion, you say and do the right things automatically.

Even advanced persuaders need to return to the basics again and again, just as pro athletes do. Whatever their sport, when each training season begins, the true superstars practice the basics right next to the rookies.

So in case we didn't mention it already, do the exercises.

But enough lecturing.

It's time to have some fun and begin your journey.

---

**Unconscious Competence is the ability
to do something effortlessly,
without thinking about it.**

---

# CHAPTER 3

# How to Become a Master Persuader

> **There are no failures. There are only experiences and information.**

You are going to learn a number of powerful persuasion techniques. At first you may experience some frustration as you try them out. Becoming a master persuader takes practice.

We will teach you specific ways to learn each technique and ingrain it into who you are so that it will become part of you.

## FOUR STEPS TO PERSUASION MASTERY

First—do the exercises.

Second—practice them in writing. This gets techniques deeper into your neurology.

Third—do them in your imagination. Pretend you are with someone with whom you are going to use a technique. Close your eyes. Imagine you are looking through your own eyes and doing the technique perfectly. You can also practice in front of a mirror, or tape record the exercise out loud so you actually get the emotions and feeling of what it is like to use this technique and be persuasive with it.

Fourth—practice these skills with people and pay attention at the same time. If you practice without observing the responses you receive, you will only occasionally hit the mark and get what you want.

David had a client with whom he was working one-on-one. The client's assignment was to meet a young woman he did not know. David video taped the experiment. The client approached a young woman and tried some persuasion techniques. He did not notice that they were not having the effect he wanted. Instead of getting to know this woman, she became hostile and told him to leave her alone.

When David replayed the video tape for his client, he showed how, at first, her cheeks reddened slightly. Her body language became more protective. Frustrated, she became extremely angry at his continued aggressiveness.

The event could have turned out differently if the client had noticed her initial reactions to him.

Practice paying attention to other people's reactions and adjust your behavior. You can accomplish what you want more consistently and become many times more persuasive.

## GET OUT OF YOUR PARENTS' BASEMENT

This is the most important way to become a Master Persuader. It is also the most difficult for many people because it means getting out of their comfort zone.

As David says, "Get out of your parents' basement." There are people who are masters of their own room but they have no skills outside of where they are living. This applies to the office as well.

So go outside where the people are so you can practice these skills. Out in the world is where you gain the power, control and ability to persuade people.

## ATTAINING EXCELLENCE

There is no such thing as failure.

There is only experience and information. Information is very useful. When Thomas Edison was trying to invent the light bulb, he tried thousands of different ways, all to no avail.

But he did not consider these efforts failures. When questioned about them by a reporter, he said he had discovered thousands of ways not to make a light bulb.

So go out and try some experiments that aren't so brilliant.

One reason some of you may resist is that you are afraid you will get caught doing the technique. Don't worry. People won't know what you are doing.

Think of it as a lighthearted social experiment. Have fun and keep your sense of humor intact.

There is no failure. Only experience and information.

## ENLIST YOUR UNCONSCIOUS MIND

Your unconscious mind is extremely powerful. It controls every aspect of your physical being from keeping your heart beating to digesting food and turning it into new cells.

Your unconscious also remembers everything you have ever experienced—in complete detail. It is also a source of inspiration, creativity, insights and intuition.

It can help you to succeed while warning you of potential problems. Unfortunately, few people listen to it. In part, this is because it speaks softly, often in dreams, using metaphors and symbols. Sometimes it just sends us a feeling about a person or opportunity. We are so focused on day-to-day events that we have forgotten it is there, ready to help us. Instead we rely on cell phones, memos, and meetings for information and ideas. There is often so much clutter in our minds that we no longer hear its voice or see the fleeting images it paints for us.

When we ignore its communication for too long, it stops sending.

Wouldn't you do the same if every time you tried to speak with someone they turned and walked away?

You can reconnect with your unconscious mind.

Take a few minutes every day to greet your unconscious mind. Welcome it like an old friend. Apologize for not listening to it and promise you will pay attention to whatever it comes up with in the form of intuition, dreams and inspiration.

Do this every day and soon you will have an open channel of communication.

You will be amazed by the results.

# CHAPTER 4

# Foundations of Persuasion

## OUTCOMES

In order to persuade someone, you must first have an outcome in mind. That is, determine in advance what you want to persuade that person to do.

We touched on this at the beginning of the book. All of us have dreams and wishes. We often call them goals, but usually they're just wishful thinking.

Goals must be written down.

In 1953 a study was done on the members of the graduating class of a prestigious university. Only 3% of them had written goals for their lives. The people conducting the study followed the fortunes of that graduating class. Twenty years later, the 3% that had written goals had outperformed financially the other 97%. If you were to average that out, each person with a goal had accumulated almost 33 times as much money as a counterpart without goals.

One of the major reasons most people don't get what they want out of life is that they never took the time to decide what they really want. They have fleeting wishes, fantasies, and dreams.

For our purposes, let's consider goals as the broad strokes.

Outcomes are similar but they are more specific. In terms of persuasion, you are looking for or trying to reach for smaller chunks of the big picture.

Let's say your goal is to be the top real estate agent in your office.

To reach that goal, your outcome might be to list one house every week. Within that outcome are smaller and smaller outcomes that you must be aware of. For example, you need to determine how many people you are going to need to talk to every day. With each person you meet, your first outcome should be to establish rapport with them (more about that soon).

You also have to qualify each couple or person to make sure they have a house they want to list. Within that outcome may be smaller outcomes, such as all of the members must agree to list the house and to list it with you.

To be a master persuader, you must know what you are going after and be able to measure how close you are getting. This is part of what we call sensory acuity, or the ability to see, hear, and feel the results you are getting (more about this, too).

Knowing what outcomes you want will give you magnitudes of persuasive ability.

What outcomes do you want from Power Persuasion?

> **To be a master persuader, you must know what you are going after and be able to measure how close you are getting.**

EXERCISE: Get a piece of paper. At the top of it write what is most important to you about learning Power Persuasion.

Once you've done that, write a small sentence or paragraph about what that will give you.

Next, write what that second thing will give you that is even more important.

Then write what that third thing will give you that is still more important.

Finally, write down what the fourth thing gives you.

Look at this answer and ask yourself, ultimately, when you have that fifth thing fully and completely, what does that give you that is more important than all the others before it? Write it down.

Look at this answer and think about it and what it means to you. It is your core value in learning persuasion. It is the reason above all others that drives you to want to master the art of persuasion.

Keep this central value in mind as you read the book and do the exercises. This is your motivation for doing the work.

## SENSORY ACUITY

Sensory Acuity is a skill. It starts when you stop thinking about yourself, worrying if you are performing the technique correctly, and paying attention to the other person. When you do this, you can notice things. If what you say has put someone in touch with some sort of emotion, it shows. Commonly, the cheeks start to flush slightly. He may look away and stare off somewhere. His eyes may begin to water.

At this point you know something powerful is going on. It may be that he is feeling sentimental or nostalgic. Or he might be reliving some painful experience. Such information is extremely useful.

If the emotion is positive, continue what you are doing. If you are drawing out negative feelings, change course or risk alienating the other person.

If you are not sure how someone is feeling, you must have more information before going any further.

Ask that person very directly: "Tell me, what are your thoughts on this?"

Once he answers, you will know whether you are getting closer to what you want, or further away, and can adjust tactics accordingly.

If you are trying to get someone to see the negative consequences of not doing what you are suggesting, then you'll want to reinforce negative feelings. Then show them how your product can create positive feelings.

Say you're selling life insurance. If your prospect doesn't have it, and he were to pass away, leaving his family in poverty, you would want to reinforce that image. Then tell him how your product can solve the dilemma, thus creating positive feelings for your product.

If you want to sell a gym membership, you can move someone towards the positive feelings she'll have from looking slim, having more energy and getting admiring looks.

Reinforcing negative emotions is a great way to motivate someone away from something. Reinforcing positive feelings will move someone toward something.

## THE TRUTH ABOUT PEOPLE

We are all motivated by emotions, not logic.

You will be persuasive to the degree that you show someone how your product, service or idea will help free them from painful emotions and reinforce positive ones.

EXERCISE: When you are with another person, imagine for a moment what it would be like to be that person with her particular body and her particular life experiences, without any of your own assumptions about what they are.

## UP TIME

In NLPspeak, when you use your sensory acuity you are in Up Time.

The opposite of Up Time is Down Time, when all of your awareness and focus is internal.

Scientists have determined that we can only pay conscious attention to five to nine things at a time. When using Power Persuasion, if you are concerned over whether you are doing the techniques correctly, it takes away from those seven things, plus or minus two, that you can focus on. It moves you closer to Down Time.

In order to be an effective persuader, you must be in Up Time and get out of your own thinking and pay attention to the other person.

## RAPPORT

What is rapport, and why is it so important?

Rapport is the foundation of persuasion.

Rapport is probably the most powerful persuasion tool you can have in any setting.

With rapport, everything is possible. Without it, nothing is possible.

We've all had an experience of interacting with someone where there is a sense of liking each other. It is easier to like someone when you have rapport, but liking someone is not the same thing as rapport. In fact, you can create rapport with someone you don't like. Nor is it necessary for them to like you in order to create rapport.

Rapport is not so much liking as it is responsiveness. You've interacted with people who've been aggressive, and you responded aggressively. The two of you go back and forth in a dance of hostility. Believe it or not, that is a form of rapport, but probably not the kind you're looking for.

You've heard the phrase, "People like people who are like themselves." It is easier to have rapport with someone who may share such similarities as culture, education, height and hair color. But what happens when people from different cultures with different hair coloring interact?

> **With rapport, everything is possible.**
> **Without it, nothing is possible.**

How do you develop rapport with someone who is very different from you?

You become like that person on much subtler levels. Rapport is created by some of the things you do, by what you say, and how you say it.

Rapport can have a very powerful effect on people, so much so that once you have established it with someone, you may not need any of the other techniques in this book. When this happens, you are performing with elegance.

Elegance is producing the biggest result with the least amount of effort.

Rapport can allow you to interact so effectively with someone that you become friends in a very short time. If that is what you are seeking, great. However, if you are trying to make a sale, you may get so distracted talking about other things that you forget the reason for your visit and walk out empty handed. So remember your outcome.

> **Elegance is producing the biggest
> result with the least amount of effort**

## CREATING RAPPORT

The biggest secret of Power Persuasion is to first cast the spell on yourself. Think about what it is like to be in rapport with yourself, so that when you see people who are in rapport with each other, you'll recognize it.

### ALWAYS USE THESE SKILLS ON YOURSELF

They will give you control of yourself. And ultimately, when you have control over yourself, controlling and persuading other people is easy, and often unnecessary.

> **When you have control over yourself,
> controlling and persuading other people is easy,
> and often unnecessary.**

## CASTING YOUR FIRST SPELL

To gain that sense of self-control, you are going to cast a monster spell on yourself so that you have even more elegance in doing just the slightest amount to make a change in yourself. When you can do this, persuasion will be effortless.

EXERCISE: Do this exercise after you have attempted any sort of persuasion, with or without these techniques.

Think about a time when you tried to persuade or influence somebody, or a group, and it didn't work out as well as you wanted. Take some time to really think about that moment. Be sure you're really back there, seeing what you saw, hearing what you heard, and feeling what you felt.

Once you are really in that moment again, imagine stepping out of your body and looking at yourself. You're not looking at that person through your eyes any more. You are looking at you attempting to influence this other person.

This is called a disassociated state.

As you see yourself doing what you are doing, make notes about the things you would like to improve or change. Maybe you want to change something you really messed up on. That's OK. In this disassociated state, you can observe yourself honestly and without emotion.

You can tell from this perspective what needs to be improved. Think about how you would improve it.

Now, go back into that first you, the one trying to do the persuading. Become associated with the experience again. Look through your own eyes. Hear your own voice as you speak. Relive that incident, but doing it RIGHT this time. Make the picture brighter. See the person or group responding the way you want.

Taking time to do this after each encounter is one of your most valuable tools for learning persuasion quickly.

## OUTCOME INSIGHTS

As we mentioned before, it critical to know your outcome in any situation. What outcomes do you want from learning these skills? Do you want to be a more effective salesperson? Do you want a more active social life? Perhaps you want to be able to interact with people on a much more personal level. Maybe you want a sense of control and power.

Take some time to think about what outcomes you desire.

EXERCISE: Go out and affect people in a way that makes them feel good, with the least amount of interaction. Your outcome for this exercise is to simply make someone smile.

You can do this with the clerk at a checkout stand. Look them in their eyes and smile and say "Thank you."

This exercise is designed for those of you who do not have a lot of experience with influence and persuasion. If you are already in a sales position, let making someone smile be your first outcome anyway. Giving someone a reason to smile is never a waste of time.

EXERCISE: When you get back home, mentally relive the previous exercise. Be in the situation and then disassociate from yourself so that you are again looking at you attempting to make someone smile. Notice what you did and how you could have done it better. Then go back inside the you having the experience and reenact the situation doing everything perfectly.

## INSTANT RAPPORT

Now it's time to learn some specific techniques that can help you create rapport with just about anyone in a matter of seconds. Two of the most basic and easiest to master are Mirroring and Matching.

## MIRRORING

Mirroring is doing the same types of body behaviors as someone else as though you are looking at yourself in a mirror. When you are facing someone, if they cross their left leg, you cross your right leg, in effect creating a mirror image of their body position. If the person you are with leans to the right in their chair, you lean to your left, again creating a mirror image.

WARNING: Do not mirror someone immediately. Wait three to five seconds and then gradually move. If you mirror someone immediately, she will think you are mimicking her and become offended.

If you adjust your body gradually, people will not notice what you are doing. But you have to mirror them exactly.

## MATCHING

Matching is doing the same thing that somebody else is doing with their body. If she crosses her left leg, you cross your left leg, and so on, after waiting three to five seconds.

Some of you may not feel comfortable mirroring and matching another person. We don't care.

It is not how comfortable you feel that matters but how comfortable you make the other person feel. If you are not willing to feel uncomfortable, consider the unspoken message of not being willing to mirror and match: "I am only willing to be with you just so much; I am not comfortable enough with you to give up myself."

Ask yourself this question: "Do I want to be someone that other people feel comfortable around?"

---

**Be willing to be a little uncomfortable in order to make other people more comfortable with you.**

---

EXERCISE: Look around at people who are in deep conversation. Notice how they tend to have the same sort of motions and body positions. If one leans forward, in a short time, the other one will too. People who are in rapport tend to subconsciously adopt the body positions of each other. Also notice which ones are not in rapport. This will help you become more aware of when your rapport techniques are working.

David remembers a time when he was in conversation with a man. They were both facing the same direction. All of a sudden both of them shifted their right foot and kicked out their left foot in unison. David almost began to laugh. What he knew that the other man did not is that they were in deep conscious rapport about a subject that was meaningful to both of them.

EXERCISE: Remember a time when you were in rapport with someone. Do you remember your body position and that of the other person? Chances are they were very similar.

## RAPPORT IS SOMETHING YOU PRACTICE CONSCIOUSLY AT FIRST UNTIL IT BECOMES AUTOMATIC

EXERCISE: One way to learn the power of matching is by doing the exact same things that other people are doing. Start noticing people and observe their body positions. You can do this with total strangers across a crowded room. Pick someone out and match their body position exactly. You don't have to interact with them. Don't glare at them. Just see what develops. Quite often, the person you are matching will look your way and perhaps even smile. They won't know why. But you will.

EXERCISE: Repeat the above exercise and add this next step. Ask yourself, "What would I be thinking if I were this person sitting in this position?"

Several years ago Dan took a class in rapport skills. Without telling the class why, the instructor had people pair off. One person in each pair was told to think intently about something. The partner then matched the other person's body position.

After a few minutes, the instructor asked the people doing the matching to guess what their partner was thinking about.

Almost every one of the "guessers" were able to tell the tone, if not the content, of the partner's thoughts and mood. That is, we could tell if he or she was thinking about something joyful or sad, angry or soothing. Some people were able to actually sense the specific topic, such as worrying about a child's health.

As you become more adept at matching, you may be surprised to find out how often you get an understanding of someone's mood. Many people can indeed detect each other's thoughts.

As you practice these new skills, take into account the situation and surroundings. In social settings, mirroring is easier to do covertly because we all tend to do it naturally anyway.

Rapport techniques work because on a subconscious level, the other person is thinking, "He's just like me."

> **Always wait three to five seconds before gradually beginning to mirror and match.**

EXERCISE: People often move their hands during conversation. When you are talking with someone, notice how they move their hands. When it is your turn to speak, gesture in the same way (three to five seconds after you start speaking).

## BE A BETTER CONVERSATIONALIST

Doing the rapport techniques helps you get out of your own head. Many people tend to have anxiety in social or business situations because they are unsure of what to say or do. They are always internalizing instead of being truly aware of what other people are doing. Their minds are cluttered with unnecessary worries such as "What should I say to her that won't sound stupid?" "Will he like me?"

As you become a rapport builder, you will actually start paying attention to other people more closely than others do. People like being paid attention to in that way. They will want to spend more time with you or be more open to your business propositions.

In order to reach this level, you have to be willing to go out and make a few mistakes and learn from them. You will not be perfect initially. Don't expect to be. At the same time, you will probably be delightfully surprised that nobody catches you doing your rapport exercises.

## VAK

VAK stand for stands for Visual-Auditory-Kinesthetic.

Most of us are blessed with five senses—sight, sound, touch, taste and smell.

The rapport skills in this book, as well as many of the other persuasion techniques, are based on Neurolinguistic Programming, better known as NLP.

NLP was developed by Richard Bandler and John Grinder a few decades ago when they began studying the relationship between the brain and language.

Bandler and Grinder found that everybody has a preferred sensory mode, and the language they use reflects how their brain processes information.

People who are highly visual think in pictures. In conversation they might say "I see what you mean" or "It's clear to me that…" or "That's a bright idea."

Auditory people process the sounds of things. They want to verbalize their thoughts. "That sounds good," "It rings true," "I hear what you're saying," are some of the thing they might say.

Kinesthetic people are into their feelings. Literally. They want something to "feel good." They want to "get a handle" on an idea. Or they might have "a gut feeling" about something. They also prefer to touch or handle things rather than look at them or talk about them.

A very small percentage of people process smell and taste as their primary sense mode. There are so few of them that we will focus on VAK.

Please keep in mind that from time to time we all switch primary sensory modes or combine them, but one will usually be predominate.

## USING VAK

Understanding sensory modes will help you increase rapport.

You will do this by matching the language that other people use. Not only does this help create rapport, it also promotes better understanding of your ideas.

Not matching their language patterns can lead to miscommunication and even hostility because you are speaking two different languages. It's like going to Germany and refusing to speak German.

A Visual may want you to "See my point of view" while an Auditory wants you to "Hear what I'm saying." Two different sensory modes. Two different languages.

> **Matching sensory mode increases rapport and understanding.**

EXERCISE: Make a list of VAK words and phrases you've heard through the years. Review your list often to remind yourself what they are so you will notice them in conversation and adapt what you say.

EXERCISE: Here's a chance to eavesdrop and not feel guilty. During your day, listen to conversations that other people are having and pay attention to the sensory modes they are using.

EXERCISE: During a conversation, listen for VAK cues and start reflecting them back to the other person. Notice their reaction.

Using VAK is especially helpful in sales or when making a presentation.

Visual people want to see pictures of the product or, if possible, the product itself. They find graphs and charts more convincing than the words you say.

An Auditory will prefer to hear what you have to say and will note how you say it. Do you speak with an air of confidence and authority, or does your voice betray uncertainty, fear or deception?

Kinesthetics will want to touch the product or hold the brochure or chart. Let them do this. Do not yank it out of their hands. If you need to point out something on the brochure, have an extra one for yourself or ask them to flip to a certain page.

## VOICE MATCHING

You can also create rapport by matching the rate at which someone speaks, as well as the tone and volume.

## SPEED

First, listen to how fast someone speaks and then gradually adjust how fast you talk to match them. Speed up to keep pace with the rapid-fire speech of a New Yorker and slow down when you hear that languid Southern drawl. Not only does it make people feel more like you (which is rapport), it also helps them process information at a rate they are comfortable with.

Visuals speak quickly because they are seeing pictures in their heads, and they want to keep pace with the ever-changing images.

Auditories tend to speak at a moderate pace and with a more sonorous voice.

Kinesthetics speak extremely slowly as they assess their feelings and gather their thoughts. They like something that grabs them. They like it when something begins to take shape. They appreciate ideas that have a solid texture, that they can wrap their ideas and thoughts around.

You can avoid frustrating people, especially clients, by matching the speed at which they talk.

## TONE

Few of us speak in a monotone. Our voices go up and down in tone during conversation. Matching that rhythm will also increase rapport.

## VOLUME

Notice the volume at which other people speak and match it. When someone talks in a loud, booming voice, you do the same. Soften your own voice with someone who speaks a low volume. Remember, the idea is to make the other person feel comfortable, not you.

EXERCISE: When you are alone, practice speaking slowly at first, then more rapidly and build up speed going faster and faster. We seldom practice speaking except when in front of people. This exercise will help you develop the facility of being flexible with your speech, without the embarrassment of doing it in front of somebody. Do this with a tape recorder because it will make you keep talking. We have the tendency to stop and think when not under pressure, so put a little pressure on yourself with the recorder.

EXERCISE: Listen for tonality, the highs and lows of other people's voices. Do they have a slight inflection in their voice when excited? Also notice the rhythm of how they go up and down. You will hear a pattern developing. Try adjusting your rhythm to match theirs.

## ACCENTS

You either love them or hate them. Either way, matching someone's accent is a great way to increase rapport. This is a little tougher than the other forms of voice matching, but well worth the effort. The key to success with accents is to listen to the vowels. If you decide to do accent matching, it is important to change gradually during the conversation.

Once you master someone else's accent, she will find it extremely flattering. It is a sign that you are becoming acutely sensitive to someone else. When you match accents, it gives people a sense of "being known," which is something we all want down deep.

EXERCISE: Go out and get in conversations with people and match them in every way possible With practice you will notice the subtle changes in how people respond to you

## BREATHING RAPPORT

One of the most elegant and powerful ways to increase rapport is by matching the rate at which someone breathes. Breathing is essential to life. It is an intimate act that we do every minute of our existence. When you breathe like another person, you are matching them on a primordial level.

There are two elements to observe: the rate or rhythm of breathing and the depth of breathing. Does that person next to you take quick breaths or long ones? Do they breathe high in the chest or draw the air down deep into their lungs?

Please don't stare or do anything inappropriate, but notice how people's chests move in and out as they breathe.

## A WORD OF CAUTION

Rapport techniques work because they cause you to become more like the person you want to influence. In a way, you are stepping into their body. And the more you become like that person *the more you become like that person, in every way.* This means that you may take on some of the emotions he is feeling at the moment. You may also even take on any physical pain or other health issues that person is experiencing.

So before you begin to establish rapport with someone, be sure you really want to be like them, if only for the moment.

EXERCISE: Go out and practice your rapport techniques. Notice the subtle changes in how people respond.

---

**Developing Sensory Acuity will help
you determine how well you are doing.**

## PACING AND LEADING

If you have been doing the exercises you should now be able to take your persuasion skills to the next level. You are beginning to do more than create rapport; you are gaining influence.

So far, you have been doing what is called Pacing, by mirroring and matching.

The next step in Power Persuasion is to begin to Lead.

In order to lead, you must test the depth of rapport.

Say that the person you are pacing has shifted his weight to his right foot and you have matched him for about 30 to 60 seconds. You have used your sensory acuity to determine that rapport has been established. Gradually shift your weight to your left foot. If the rapport is strong, he will start to shift his weight to the left foot.

If he does shift, then, one by one, gradually change some other aspects of your body position. Keep changing to the point where he doesn't follow any more. Start pacing again and test the rapport by leading.

When you are able to lead someone, you are actually influencing them. That is the power of rapport.

EXERCISE: Pace someone and then make small changes to test rapport. As soon as they stop following you, resume pacing and then practice leading.

> **Once you've established rapport,
> you can begin to lead other people.**

## POWER RAPPORT

On several levels, this technique is much simpler than other rapport techniques, but it's also much more advanced. It works by creating a model that your conscious mind may find reasonable and doable even if it is a bit "out there." Remember, people like people who are like themselves. And who could be more like someone than themselves?

In this technique you are going to imagine being the other person talking to himself. Here's how:

1) When you engage in some interaction with another person, imagine that there is an exact duplicate of him just in front of you facing him.

2) Imagine stepping out of your body and "stepping into" the duplicate and becoming him. If a third person could participate in this hallucination they would see the person you're talking to talking to a duplicate of himself!

3) Use all your senses to imagine what it's like as you look through his eyes at himself, hear his own words coming from his mouth and move around in his body.

4) Ask yourself several questions as you do this. What does it feel like to be this gender (if it's not your own)? How warm is it in this body? What are the feelings and emotions I'm feeling in this body?

This technique works because it forces your mind to match EVERYTHING in that person's experience.

When you do this for the first time, it can be a bit overwhelming. You may even lose sight of your outcome. Don't worry. Everything you learn here is a skill, and with practice you will improve greatly.

WARNING: As we mentioned before, be careful who you step into! Would you really want to step into the mind of a paranoid schizophrenic or someone in chronic pain?

# CHAPTER 5

# Values

Values are the things that are most important to us. Values move us through the world

When you are talking to people, notice those moments when they just sort of light up, when they come alive. Notice the words they use. In those moments, it is highly likely that they are revealing their highest values in those words.

Each of us has different values. Some thirst for adventure while others prefer the comforts of home. One man wants to build his body while "A girl's just gotta have fun."

In addition to having different values, we each have a hierarchy of values. One value will mean more than all of the other values combined.

Learning another person's values is a powerful persuasion tool. Showing someone how your product, your idea, or you yourself will fulfill their highest value, that thing they treasure most, can make you and your offer irresistible.

EXERCISE: Write down the things that you value most. These are the things that motivate you. Next time you think you need a little extra push to get yourself going, think about how your project will help fulfill one or more of your values.

## USING VALUES TO PERSUADE

How do you learn someone's values?
Ask them.

Once you've established rapport, they will tell you what is important to them. People love to talk about what they cherish most.

If you are in a sales situation, you will also need to know what your prospect's criteria are. Criteria are related to function (cheap, fast, best, state-of-the-art, etc.).

Show and tell the prospect how your product meets those criteria.

Don't try to sell based on what is important to you.

If you're selling stereos and the customer says she wants something that will fit on her desk, don't drone on about all the great bass your systems have. Show her something that will fit on her desk.

Once you've met criteria, it's time to seek out values.

Let's say you're selling database software to a small business owner.

Ask her: "What's important to you in a database?"

Notice, you do not ask *why*. Asking *why* will cause people to justify their reasoning

*Why* elicits a conscious response. *What* reveals an unconscious response, which means you are reaching someone on a deeper level.

Let's go back to the original example of database software.

"What's important in database software?" you ask.

"I want something to give me an overview," she responds.

"What's important about an overview?" you gently nudge.

"It helps me get more organized."

"What's important about being organized?"

"I can do my inventory reports faster," she says wistfully.

"What's important about doing reports faster?"

"I can go home earlier and spend more time with my family." She smiles and leans back in her chair. Her eyes light up as they drift to a photograph on her desk.

You have discovered what is truly important to her: spending time with her family.

In order to get to this highest value, you usually have to go four or five levels deep, but once you've touched on what makes someone tick, persuading is easy.

All you have to do is show this business owner how your database software will give her the organization she needs. Tell her about how fast it is and how she will finish her work earlier so she can "Go home earlier and spend more time" with her family.

Usually, the highest value will be just a word or phrase— security, confidence, peace of mind. Everyone is different and every situation is different. In another context, our business owner might have a totally different value.

If you were selling her a car, safety might be her highest priority because she has children. You would then build your pitch around how safe the car is.

Whenever you hear what someone's highest value is, make a mental note so you can repeat it back exactly as they stated it.

If a prospect tells you his highest value is financial security don't say that your insurance package offers financial freedom. Tell him how it will give him financial security.

You must use his words because you are dealing with his realty, not yours. It is his reality you are trying to influence, not yours.

Once you show someone how your product, service or idea will fulfill their highest value, you seldom have to close. Your "close" is nothing more than saying, "As you think about financial security, and you see how this insurance can give it to you, does it sound like something you'd like to do?"

A note about closing. It has often been presented as a way of arguing your prospect into buying. But if you fulfill their highest value, there is no argument. She may have additional questions. If so, all you have to do is tie your responses to her highest value.

But you must have sensory acuity. Watch for those signs that show deep emotion. Listen to those key words that underscore what someone is feeling.

EXERCISE: When talking with people with whom you have rapport, start asking "what is important about" questions to learn their deepest values. It can improve all of your relationships when you know what people truly want because you can stop guessing about what will make a friend, lover or business associate feel better.

**If what you want someone to do
fulfills their highest values,
it's almost impossible for them to say no.**

# CHAPTER 6

# The Power of States

States move people to action. Despite what we tell ourselves, we do things for emotional reasons, not logical ones. We may justify our actions with logic but the true reason we act is because we feel strongly about something.

Imagine what it would be like to induce the emotional states that move people to action. It is the power called State Elicitation. If you can do this, you have true persuasive power.

## ELICITING STATES

The first key to eliciting a state in someone is to create it in yourself.

If you want a prospect to buy something, create a buying state in yourself. Fall in love with your product.

If you want to influence someone romantically, start to feel a deep state of connection with that other person. Create rapport and begin leading. If you go somewhere emotionally, she or he will tend to go there too. Use your sensory acuity to know when this is happening.

Then ask some very simple questions. You might ask, "Do you remember the last time you felt romantic feelings for someone? What was it you saw or heard or felt?" Remember VAK? Listen for the sensory modalities.

If you have created rapport, she will tell you what modality or modalities affected her. It may have been the way he looked in her eyes or the way he spoke her name. If you can duplicate this experience, you have a high probability of moving her towards romance.

Please use this technique only if you are sincere about wanting to win someone's affection. Nobody deserves to be manipulated, or worse, have their heart broken by a man or woman who is just out for a good time. We remind you again that what you sow you shall reap.

## ELICITING STATES FOR SALES

Eliciting states is a great way to make sales.

After you've established rapport, ask your prospect, "Have you ever seen something and really wanted it?"

At this point, just shut up and listen. Maybe he won't say much. Maybe he'll talk and talk. If this happens, just listen. He is giving you information you need to hear.

If he only says a few words, or even just "yeah," ask for more information.

You might ask, "When you knew you wanted it, how did you know?"

He will give you information in sensory terms, something he saw, heard or felt.

He may also tell you such things as how he came about the process.

This is another way to elicit states. Ask someone how he reached a decision to buy. Shut up and listen. He will tell you his decision-making process.

### THIS WILL ONLY HAPPEN IF YOU HAVE ALREADY ESTABLISHED RAPPORT

At this point all you have to do is describe your product in terms of his process. It may not be your process, but that doesn't matter. It is the buyer's process that matters.

It is vital to match the prospect's process exactly. When you do, it is like having the combination to their brain.

For example, he might say he saw the object and it brought this warm feeling and then he said something to himself about wanting the object. If you're selling cars, you would feed back to the prospect something like, "As you look at this new car, you can think about the warm feelings you will have sitting in it, and you might say to yourself: 'I want this car.'"

You are reflecting back to him his exact decision-making process for buying something. He almost has to buy. To do otherwise would be to deny his very being. Eliciting states is that simple and that powerful.

> **Knowing someone's decision-making process is like having the combination to their brain.**

EXERCISE: Talk with someone who bought something important recently. Ask them how they reached the decision to buy and listen for the VAK sequence.

## CONGRUITY

In NLP terms, you have Congruity when your inner states match your outer actions and speech

Have you ever met someone who seemed charming and sincere, yet for some reason, you did not trust him? It was probably because his inner states, his true feelings or motivation, did not match his demeanor. Though he said and did the right things, you felt uneasy about opening up your wallet or heart to him.

That person was incongruous. As part of developing sensory acuity, become aware of when your inner mind is giving you such clues about other people. It may be something you see, an inner voice or a gut feeling. Whenever you get such a message, pay attention.

At the same time, if you want to be a Power Persuader you must develop your own congruity. You have to believe, really live and believe, what you are trying to convince other people to do. People who are congruent with their inner motivations and outer actions can be very charismatic, so much so that others will willingly do what they ask.

If you are in sales but don't like your product, find another one that you can be proud of. You'll make more money because you will transfer that sense of belief to your customers.

Want to ask out that person you've had your eye on? Make sure you are congruent. Align yourself with the positive intentions you have and you'll more likely get a positive response.

---

**You have congruity when your
inner states match your actions.**

---

EXERCISE: Paint a picture in your mind that has you already having done all of the exercises and having learned all the skills. Hear the words you say resonate inside you. Most of all, start to feel very powerful. Have a gut feeling that says: "I can do this." As you get that feeling, take a moment to look out into your future, six months or a year from now, having practiced each one of the exercises and perhaps gone even further to learn these linguistic skills and patterns.

Create that future of being a powerful persuader now. Practice practice practice.

Your ability will grow a hundred-fold, maybe a thousand-fold.

Remember, there are no failures, only information.

# CHAPTER 7

# Hypnotic Influence

What is hypnosis and why are these techniques hypnotic?

Some of you may be concerned about the idea of using hypnosis to influence people. Somehow, it may seem wrong or even evil. We commend your integrity. However, the fear is unfounded.

Before we address the hypnotic aspect of Power Persuasion, it is important for you to understand what hypnosis is and what it is not.

Hypnosis is not a form of mind control. It is not an occult power.

When you are in a hypnotic trance, you are usually aware of your surroundings. Your mind has not gone anywhere. Many people enter hypnosis so deeply that they believe that they have fallen asleep, but they have not.

Hypnosis is a natural state that we all enter several times a day. Daydreaming is a form of hypnotic state. Thinking intently about a problem or goal is a hypnotic state. Writing a story, creating a piece of art, playing a musical instrument can all lead to a hypnotic trance.

One of the most common situations in which we enter a trance is watching a movie or television. Advertisers know this which is why they pay big money to sell you their products on television.

Fortunately, hypnosis is primarily used for positive purposes such as to lose weight, stop smoking, gain self-confidence, reduce stress, stop pain, remove phobias and much more.

## WHAT MODERN HYPNOSIS CAN DO FOR YOU

As a practical definition, hypnosis is a relaxed state of focused attention. It usually involves what is called an altered state of consciousness.

During your normal waking activity, your brain emits a series of waves in rapid succession. These are known as Beta waves. When you are relaxed, your brain produces fewer waves, or beats, per minute. These slower waves are called Alpha waves. If you are deeply relaxed, you have extremely slow waves called Theta waves. The slowest waves, called Delta, are emitted when you are in deep sleep.

Alpha and Theta waves are associated with the hypnotic state.

Decades ago, the hypnotist might have the subject (you) focus on an object, such as a gold watch hanging from a chain, swinging like a pendulum. There is nothing inherently hypnotic about a watch, although we do seem to be obsessed with time. The watch merely served as a focal point of concentration.

While the subject's eyes followed the watch, the hypnotist would give them suggestions for relaxation which would help them enter the hypnotic state.

In modern hypnosis, the hypnotist uses verbal suggestions for relaxation. He or she may have soothing music playing in the background.

The reason that the hypnotist helps you enter a relaxed state is that you become more open to suggestions that you want to become part of your belief system.

This leads us to an important question. Can someone under hypnosis be made to do things they would not ordinarily do?

The answer is no. But sometimes yes.

First of all, in a clinical setting, the client and hypnotist act in cooperation. There is a high level of trust. Although the hypnotist is giving suggestions for relaxation, the client is really hypnotizing himself. The hypnotist is acting as a guide to help him enter a relaxed state.

A skilled hypnotist also knows how to construct the most effective suggestions to help you make changes you want. If you don't like what the hypnotist is saying to you, or if you begin to feel uncomfortable with the process you can end it by simply opening your eyes.

You are in control at all times.

Here comes the yes part.

Many of the Power Persuasion techniques that you will learn induce a mild trance in people. When this happens, they are very suggestible to things that fit their character and values.

You could not use these techniques to make an honest person rob a bank.

But you can use Power Persuasion to sell a business owner a computer. He will likely buy from you because that does not violate his values. He was going to buy a computer from somebody anyway. If he is not tech savvy, you can even sell him upgrades he will never use. In this case, he doesn't know that one aspect of his values (getting a fair deal) has been violated, so he will follow your suggestions.

The down side is, later on, once he realizes that you've suckered him, he will not do business with you again.

So use these techniques with discretion and honor. Honest business is smart business. The same holds true for personal relationships.

# CHAPTER 8

# Military Linguistic Patterns

Anyone who's ever enlisted knows how persuasive those military recruiters in their pressed uniforms can be.

And let's face it, they have to be.

Military service, though honorable, is not the most benefit-rich product that someone could sell. When you enlist, you agree to a four-year commitment. During this time, you give up your freedom. You must do what you are told no matter how much you might not like it or the people who are telling you to do it.

This is ironic because the majority of those who enlist are young men who sign up at a time in life when many of them tend to be the most rebellious.

Military recruiters sell a product that requires a great deal of physical commitment and training.

Serving in the military does not pay all that well, but if you stay in for life, there are great retirement benefits.

Despite the drawbacks, people all over the nation are persuaded to join the military every day.

Those who study this dynamic have found that the top recruiters tend to use some of the same linguistic patterns on a regular basis. Now, almost all military recruiters are trained to use these patterns.

## WHAT MAKES THEM WORK

Military linguistic patterns are simple in format yet they allow you to place your outcome and deal with objections easily and quickly in a very fluid way.

But there is another key factor that makes these patterns work.

Consider the type of personality that a military recruiter has to have in order to be effective. This will help you develop some of those same qualities that makes these men and women so effective at sales. When you combine these qualities to the patterns, you will be an extremely effective Power Persuader.

First of all, you MUST use your rapport skills. Military recruiters would not be able to do what they do without establishing rapport.

Also consider the potential state of mind the recruiter maintains, part of which is a set of beliefs. One of these beliefs is that they are absolutely committed to their job. They believe what they are doing is highly important, and they are absolutely committed to doing it.

Military recruiters derive a huge amount of satisfaction and fulfillment from what they do. The most successful recruiters have done just about everything that can be done in their branch of the service prior to becoming a recruiter. They love the training and the challenge. They love the challenge of convincing people to join, which only makes sense. If you've ever tried to sell something you don't like, you'll find out how truly difficult that is.

EXERCISE: As you think about what you have just read, begin to see what it would be like to love challenge, to love an opportunity to do something that is just slightly outside of your comfort zone, and to accomplish something that seems to take on a little bit of effort and bring that feeling to life.

Another quality of military recruiters, and exceptional sales pros, is they love to be around the people they are trying to influence. In fact, they love people in general.

EXERCISE: Take a moment to feel what it's like to be around somebody and really enjoy their presence and having that warmth and feeling of rapport with them.

Let's review the fundamental qualities and beliefs of the top military recruiters

1) They love a challenge.

2) They are committed to what they are doing.

3) They like the people they are dealing with.

There are probably others but these are the three basic beliefs that the top military recruiters and salespeople have.

EXERCISE: As you think about these qualities, imagine what feelings you can bring about as you come in line with those particular beliefs. As you are doing each of these military patterns, you will find that they are tools that you can combine with all the other Power Persuasion techniques. You'll see ways that you can use these patterns in your life and how incredibly exciting that can be.

Before you learn these patterns and begin to use them, remember that you must have an outcome. Think of outcomes in terms of feelings and benefits that the person you are trying to influence will experience.

---

> **Emotional outcomes are the feelings and benefits you want the other person to experience.**

---

## THE PATTERNS

### Have you found...?

Use this phrase in constructing a question that contains or leads to your outcome.

Examples:

*Learning Power Persuasion*

"Have you found a growing sense of excitement as you consider how you're going to use these patterns in your life?"

"Have you found that as you think about being more influential that the idea of using these patterns daily in your life becomes a clearer, brighter, sharper picture than you ever thought you could possibly imagine?"

"Have you found that when you think about control, when you think about being in control of your life, about being influential, you know that it's important to learn new skills; and that as the excitement and drive grow, you can apply that excitement to this particular training?"

Notice, we did not just say: "Have you found that you want to do this?" We didn't just say: "Have you found you want to learn more?" What we asked was: "Have you found that growing sense of excitement…?"

Remember, people respond to emotions, not to thoughts, not to actions. So your outcome has to be more than just a thought or an idea. It has to be something that moves them.

*Military Recruiter*

"Have you found that in order to get the jobs that you want, you have to have the skills and training that are needed?"

Of course the answer to that is yes.

The recruiter would then say: "But you're in a Catch 22. You can't get the job without the training. Then how are you going to get the training?"

After that he would say: "Have you found a real urge to accomplish something in your life, something that has meaning? Something that's bigger than you? Now, as you think about that, let me show you how your participation in (this branch of the service) is going to help you get the training you need to really make a difference."

*More Military Examples*

"Have you found that so many of your peers are seeing the military as a viable option for career training?"

"Have you found yourself wondering what would probably be the best and most effective direction to take after high school?"

*Selling Gym Memberships* (something David used to do)

"Have you found that having a fitness program is something that a lot of your friends are committing to?"

"Have you also found that fitness memberships are something your friends are enjoying as well?"

"Have you found that your well-being just naturally comes from enjoying a fitness program?"

"Have you found that a fitness program is one of the best ways to increase your sense of well-being?"

What you will notice about this particular military pattern (and some of the others) is that it is a way of directing thought, a way of directing the conversation, and directing the other person's attention toward your outcome of developing excitement.

*In Conversation*

David has developed a much longer pattern to develop both rapport and fascination:

"I find it so interesting when you're involved in a conversation and can become so engrossed that you just begin to focus in on the subject. Have you found how people just tend to fall into that type of conversation and how rare that type of conversation we're now having really is?"

Because this is a yes or no question, they might respond in the negative. If this happens, you simply respond by saying: "Oh, not yet, huh?" Then move on quickly to the next topic.

EXERCISE: Write down your (emotional) outcomes, and then write down four specific ways you would use "have you found...?" to create those outcomes

## Would it be fair to say...?

This type of question allows you to lead the conversation because you insert your outcome in the form of a question.

Examples:

*Learning Power Persuasion*

"Would it be fair to say there is a certain growing sense of eagerness about learning and applying these military patterns?"

"Would it be fair to say that the more you learn about linguistic persuasion, the more eager you are to learn more?"

"Would it be fair to say that, based on your value to powerfully influence other people, you can find your own reasons to continue to study these military patterns?"

"Would it be fair to say that the more you study these techniques, the more you are aware of how powerful you are learning to become?"

"Would it be fair to say that traditional sales training will only get you so far?"

*Military Recruiter*

"Would it be fair to say that you really want to improve your life?"

"Would it be fair to say that you really want to take control of your life, that you want to have a sense of control, of discipline, to really build your life, to really make it worthwhile?"

"Would it be fair to say that a high school diploma is really only going to get you so far?"

*Gym Memberships*

"Would it be fair to say that a fitness program is the best way to achieve your particular goals for physical fitness?"

"Would it be fair to say that taking the time to use, nurture and develop a fitness program is a very small price to pay to have that ultimate sense of fulfillment?"

EXERCISE: Write down your (emotional) outcomes and then write down four specific ways you would use this pattern to create those outcomes.

---

**People take action because of emotions,
not thoughts.**

---

**Just suppose...**

This is a wonderful pattern. As hypnosis shows, when you have someone who is willing to "just suppose," you have them essentially in trance. When they suppose something, they are going into a deep trance where anything you are saying is true.

Why is it true? Because they are just *supposing* it is true.

Have them just suppose not only your outcome but wonderful feelings that are associated with it. Keep in mind, people are motivated by feelings, not just actions, not just thoughts, but by feelings.

Remember, if you develop rapport, if you pay attention, they're going to tell you the feelings that they want to feel. They're going to tell you their deepest values and what truly motivates them.

You want to tie these feelings to the action they are just supposing.

Examples:

*Learning Power Persuasion*

"Just suppose, for a moment, you've really mastered military patterns and the other Power Persuasion techniques, that you have a sense of control, of power and a sense of self-assuredness about what you can do and how you can influence people."

"Just suppose for a moment that you can walk into any social situation and know that you can be in charge and have control because you can rely on all of the training this book has given you because you've mastered the techniques. That's a great feeling, isn't it?"

"Just suppose for a moment that there's a time in your future when you've accomplished exactly what you want, that you've been able to be the best salesperson you want to be, to be the best influencer that you want to be. Maybe you have a political ambition or maybe you just want to communicate in a way that's effective, one that truly touches people."

*Military Recruiter*

"Just suppose for a moment that you've worked really hard to get out of your basic training, that you're in the best shape of your life, that you have a sense of pride and accomplishment about everything you've done. And as you think back on that, and you knew it was tough and you overcame it with the support of the people that are there to help you—that feels pretty good, doesn't it?"

After talking with the recruit and finding out their particular interests or areas in which they want to be trained, the recruiter would simply paint that picture.

"Just suppose for a moment, once you've got the training, something that is going to be there the rest of your life are the skills and the basic groundwork that you are going to use in any job that you have in the future. And you know they're going to be there. Just imagine that sense of satisfaction and that confidence, knowing you can walk into any situation with the training you got here. That feels pretty good, doesn't it?"

EXERCISE: Think about how you would use "just suppose..." You want to paint a colorful picture filled with emotion, ideals, and values that the person you're attempting to influence truly wants.

> **Use your rapport skills to learn people's values and incorporate them into the military patterns.**

## What would happen if (you name your outcome) because (insert their value)?

This one is also hypnotic because it too allows you to "just suppose." And you get to impose on this their particular values.

Remember, values are those things that are most important to people and move them through the world.

Examples:

*Learning Power Persuasion*

"What would happen if you really committed yourself to studying and mastering military patterns and the other Power

Persuasion techniques because you really value this sense of empowerment, this sense of control and being able to powerfully influence other people?"

"What would happen if you felt so confident in your ability that you could go out and talk to anybody because you're so well trained and because you have this ability to influence other people?"

"What would happen if you decided to commit to studying these processes because the ability to influence and having that sense of control in your life is important?"

*Military Recruiter*

"What would happen if you joined up because you want that sense of commitment, because you want that sense of contribution to society?"

"What would happen if you enlisted because you know that you'd be getting the training that you need that's going to follow you the rest of your life?"

*Gym Memberships*

"What would happen if you joined because you recognize that it will bring you closer to your fitness goals?"

"What would happen if you got a membership simply because you know it's going to make you feel good about yourself in all the ways that you like?"

## Don't (action or objection) unless you want to (name your outcome).

What you're really saying here is: "Don't object unless you want to go my way."

The interesting thing about this pattern is it ties someone into going your way. If they go your way, they go your way. If they object, they go your way.

Logically, it doesn't make any sense but as you're gaining rapport and feeding back to people their values, you're going to find this pattern has lots of power.

Examples:

*Learning Power Persuasion*

"Don't even consider hesitating studying this information unless you're absolutely committed to learning more about Power Persuasion."

"Don't even consider resting unless you know you're going to study more."

"Don't put this book down unless you want to come back to it again and again."

*Military Recruiter*

"Don't walk out of here unless you're committed to enlist."

That may be too direct, but it might work. Something softer might be:

"Don't stand up from that chair unless you know exactly what your future's going to give you."

"Don't think about this for too long unless you really want to take charge of your life and really want to have control of your future."

*Gym Membership*

"A friend of mine who's really committed to training once said 'don't even walk into a gym unless you want the health and vitality that your life is really missing.'"

EXERCISE: Write down four different actions that your prospect should not take unless he or she wants your proposition.

The next three Military Patterns are designed to overcome objections.

Note, in all three of the following patterns, you don't argue against the objection because that will cause the other person to defend his side. Instead, you are agreeing with the objection in a minor way, which validates his feelings.

Also keep in mind that skilled negotiators start by asking for much more than they want so they can make concessions along the way. This allows the person that they are negotiating with to feel that they worked for and got the best deal.

**I appreciate (intent of the objection) and what would happen if (new behavior), because (reason) I'd be willing to (concession).**

This pattern has four aspects to it:

Agree with the objection.
Introduce your outcome.
Describe the reasoning.
Tell them a small concession you're willing to make in exchange for them agreeing to your proposal.

The concession is key because it uses one of the most powerful persuasion techniques, which is Reciprocity (more about Reciprocity later).

Examples:

*Learning Power Persuasion*

"I appreciate you thinking this is a lot for you to learn. What would happen if you just studied a certain amount every day, say 15 minutes, to learn this because you realize it's important because you know it's going to give you a sense of power, of influence? If you do that, I will give you a free phone consultation."

*Military Recruiter*

"I really do appreciate your concern about the rigors of basic training. What would happen if you went through training because you knew at the end you'd be introduced to the highest quality training in the field that you're most interested in? Now, if you'd be willing to do that I would be absolutely willing to guarantee that you'd be placed in that particular field."

*Gym memberships*

"I appreciate you wanting to save money on your gym membership. What would happen if you started your program today because you wanted to, and you wanted to start losing weight and getting healthier right away? Now if you did that, I'd be willing to add one month free to your membership."

When you're using this particular military pattern, the interesting thing is you don't have to have a logical reason for them to do the new behavior. You could simply say: "I appreciate you wanting to save money. What would happen if you signed up because it's a sunny day?" ("Because it's Tuesday?" "Because it just feels good right now?") "Now if you'd do that, I'd be willing to (offer your concession)."

It's good to use logic and when you put in a reason for them to do this new behavior, it's important to find a reason that's actually of value to them, but it doesn't always have to be logical.

Let us also point out something that should be obvious. Make sure you know your product and be sure of the concessions you can offer, such as a price break or additional product or service.

EXERCISE: Write down four objections and the ways you could use this pattern to overcome them.

**Yes (you agree with the negative feature objected to), but (positive feature of your proposal) and if you're (committed to emotion/value) then (you must be committed to proposal).**

Again, you are not arguing about the objection. You are acknowledging the negative feature. But you are linking a higher value or emotion to your presentation.

This military pattern also has four components:

You agree that the feature is negative.
You mention a positive feature.
Then you mention a commitment to an emotion.
Finish with a commitment to a proposal or follow-through.

Again, this pattern does require that you understand your product and that you listen and pay attention to the prospect.

Examples:

*Learning Power Persuasion*

"I agree that learning these linguistic patterns does take time and effort, but as you know, when you put in this time and effort, it can benefit you in the long run; and if you're committed to being influential and having that sense of control in your life, then you must be committed to putting aside the time to study this."

Notice there is an agreement to the objection. People can't argue with someone who is agreeing with them. Next, you are pointing out a truism, something that is obviously true, that is positive that the prospect has to agree to. Next, you are saying that if he or she is committed to a feeling (that they've already told you about), then they must be committed to this proposal. Everything that precedes the suggestion to committing to the proposal is true, so they have to agree with the final thing that is suggested.

*Military Recruiter*

"Yes, this is a four-year commitment, but if you think about the training, if you think about the college education, if you think about the benefits that are there for you, you know there are features you can use the rest of your life. Now if you're committed to that feeling of self-improvement, that wonderful feeling of contributing to the greater society, then you must be committed to enlisting."

*Gym Memberships*

"Yes, the membership requires a monthly withdrawal from your checking account, but with it you get 24-hour availability to a gym and free training. And if you're committed to getting the changes that you admitted to, that you need, you must be committed to this program."

"Yes, the price is fixed, but the program does provide you with features you've asked for; and if you're dedicated to making the changes that will bring you closer to the stamina you want, then you'd agree that this is the fairest option."

EXERCISE: List the objections you might get as well as the emotions that your clients and prospects have that motivate them to do things that will also motivate them to buy your product or service. Once you have those, start designing this military pattern with those objections and your responses in mind.

**(Your objective) and I appreciate (future obstacles). Imagine for a moment that together we/you (overcome future obstacles) as we've/you've done in the past, don't you feel good now?**

This pattern assumes a preexisting relationship with the person you're working with, even if it's only been for a short time. It also assumes that you've worked together to overcome certain obstacles.

It is designed to create a feeling of reciprocity, a good feeling and the ability to overcome any objection that they might have. You use this pattern if someone likes what you're proposing but they say: "But what if...?" They are seeing possible future obstacles and you are helping them to overcome the roadblocks in their own mind.

There are several components:

You state your outcome

You agree with their objection

You have them imagine overcoming future obstacles as they remember doing so in the past.

Then you ask: "Don't you feel good now?"

Examples:

*Learning Power Persuasion.*

Objection: It takes time to study.

"I really want you to continue to study and continue to learn all of the language patterns that I have to offer. Some of you appreciate the fact that it takes time to study and do the exercises and to practice. I'd like you to just imagine for a moment that we are working together through this book so that you have a deep and profound understanding of these language patterns. And we will work together just as we have before. As you think about it, don't you feel good now?"

*Military Recruiter*

Objection: The recruit is concerned his family might need him.

"Jimmy, I really want you to be a part of the military, particularly this branch of the service, and I appreciate that you have concerns about your family, about being there for them. I'd like you to imagine for a moment that you and I have worked together so that if something comes up, you can respond to it just as you need to, just as we've done in the past. As you think about that, don't you feel good now?"

*Gym Membership*

Objection: Working out in public.

"I want you to enjoy your gym membership, and I appreciate your being self-conscious about working out in a public place. Imagine for a moment that you've overcome this fear, like you did while speaking in public last week. As you think about that, don't you feel good now?"

EXERCISE: Write down four objections and how you can use this military pattern to overcome them.

---

**Never argue with an objection. Instead, agree with it and point out the qualities of your product, service or idea.**

---

# CHAPTER 9

# Assorted Techniques

## RECIPROCITY PATTERN

This pattern will help you gain a sense of indebtedness. There is no specific outcome, short of making someone feel good and creating a feeling of the need for reciprocity, hence the name.

So whenever anyone says "Thank you" for something that you're doing, all you say is: "You're welcome. I'm certain that you would have done the same thing for me, wouldn't you?"

When you say this they have to agree. On an unconscious level it creates a sense of indebtedness.

## WHEN WOULD NOW BE A GOOD TIME...?

This is a very elegant pattern. You simply ask: "When would now be a good time...?" Then you insert your outcome.

Examples:

*Sales*

"When would now be a good time to go ahead and sign that contract?"

"When would now be a time to make an appointment?"

"When would now be a good time to buy this new car?"

## BECAUSE

This pattern relies on a process that the mind goes through that can be referred to as default logic. It is a type of logic that is not necessarily logical. In fact, all you really have to do is say "because." When you say "because" the mind tends to agree *because* you are giving a reason even though the reason may have nothing to do with reality.

Studies were done in which an experimenter asked to cut in line at busy copy machines. He would simply ask something along the lines of: "May I go ahead of you? I want to make some copies." Very few people said yes.

When he asked: "May I go ahead of you *because* I want to make some copies?" many people said yes.

It didn't matter that he wanted to cut in line at the copy machine *because* he wanted to make some copies. So did they. But to their subconscious minds, whatever followed the word *because* seemed like a valid reason.

## SINGLE BINDS

### The more that you X, the more that you Y.

Examples:

*Learning Power Persuasion*

"The more that you read this book, the more you want to practice each of the exercises"

*Real Estate*

"The more that you walk around this house, the more you're going to be able to see yourself living here and feeling very comfortable."

*Car Sales*

"The more you drive this car, the more you see yourself own-ing it."

### The more you X, the less you Y.

Examples:

*Learning Power Persuasion*

"The more you practice these patterns, the less insecure you will feel."

*Gym Memberships*

"The more you exercise, the less stress you will feel."

*Real Estate*

"The more time you spend in this house, the less you will like the others you've seen."

*Other Single Bind Patterns*

The sooner you X, the quicker you Y.
The more you X, the faster you Y.
The faster you X, the safer you Y.

Have fun with this pattern and see how many ways you can use it.

EXERCISE: Create four single bind patterns that you can use in your business or personal life and write them down.

## DOUBLE BINDS

This pattern is also called an Alternate Close. Double Binds are often used in sales.

Examples:

*Car Sales*

"Would you like this car in red or blue?"

*Restaurants*

"Do you want red or white wine with your meal?"

Notice that in each example the choice offered is not yes or no but *which*? This pattern presumes you are going to buy. All that's left are the details. Either way you are going to buy a car or drink some wine.

EXERCISE: Write down four double binds that you can use to be a more powerful persuader.

## FUN WITH NOMINALIZATIONS

In order to understand Nominalizations, you have to be aware of how the human mind likes to simplify things. In that simplification process, we take whole processes and turn them into a thing (a noun).

An example is the word *decision*. Someone goes through a process of *deciding*(a verb). But they turn the end result into a thing called a *decision*. In other words, what they are really doing is freezing back in time. They are treating it as something you can put in a wheelbarrow or put in your pocket.

Every time someone does this or talks about a *decision* in that context, they are taking away the process. And in so doing, the process becomes a noun instead of a verb.

Knowing this distinction can be very useful.

Suppose someone is *deciding* something. He is in the process, which he may stay in for a long time, maybe months. With nominalizations, you can bring the process to a conclusion, *a decision*.

For example, if a prospect tells you he is still *deciding* whether to buy, you might respond with: "What information do you need to *decide to buy now*?" That last phrase can be emphasized to make it an imbedded suggestion as well.

On the other hand, if he's made a *decision* (not to buy), you can turn that static thing back into a process in order to encourage him to reconsider.

You might ask: "How did you go about deciding that?" As he considers his answer, he is going back into the process of *deciding*, which allows you to apply more Power Persuasion tools to the response he gives you.

### *Creating Nominalizations*

As a general rule, any verb you can put *tion*, *sion* or *ize* on can be a nominalization. And there are others.

Examples:

| | |
|---|---|
| To Decide | Decision |
| To Experience an | the Experience |
| To Communicate | a Communication |
| To Function | a Function, the Function of |
| To Close | the Close (of a sale) |
| To Grow | Growth |
| To Accept | Acceptance |
| To Realize | Realization |
| To Doubt | a Doubt |
| To Choose | a Choice |

Here's the fun part of using nominalizations.

When you link three of them together it tends to put the person you are talking to in a mild trance because his brain is trying to link them together in a way that makes sense. Remember, when you put someone in a trance, they are open to suggestions.

To get the full effect of linking nominalizations, make an infinitive verb (to be, to run, etc.) your outcome.

Example:

"Tell me about the *doubts* about your *ability* to make a *commitment* in yourself."

When you say something like that, most people have to stop and turn their attention inside. They have to unpack the meaning of all those nominalizations. While their brain is occupied, you slip in what you want them to do. In the example above, you want them *to make a commitment*.

### Constructing Nominalization Chains

You start with a nominalization and you connect it with one of three words: *of, about* or *how*. Precede the next nominalization with either *your* or *the*. You often finish with an infinitive verb as your outcome.

If you were to diagram the basic pattern it would look like this:

**Nominalization** of, about, how your/the **Nominalization** infinitive verb

OR:

Your/the **Nominalization** of, about, how **Nominalization** infinitive verb

Examples:

*Learning Power Persuasion*

"I hope you can begin to appreciate your acceptance of the eagerness to learn Power Persuasion."

*Relationships*

"Notice the process of your choice to connect powerfully in this relationship."

This pattern looks odd when written down, but it can be very effective when speaking to people. It will confuse them and eventually they will ask you what you mean. At this point, you can suggest what they should do (your outcome).

So what you are doing is making a broad statement with lots of nominalizations in it, and then you end it with something very simple and very direct that can be easily understood. For example, suppose you have an outcome to lock in certainty to achieve a particular outcome.

You could say: "The more you may sense any doubt in your ability to commit, the easier grows the certainty, the single-mindedness to create this outcome. *You know you can do it.*"

You use that long phrase and end it with something simple: "You know you can do it."

Because the mind doesn't like confusion, doesn't like having to hunt for meaning, it automatically accepts that very simple phrase (at the end) that is given to it.

*Nominalizations and the Single Bind*

You may have noticed that these sentences are using a single bind format—the more that you X, the more that you Y.

Keep in mind that when creating a single bind, there are two sections to it. The first part is the more you X. The second is the more you Y. What we're doing is using that nominalization formula in both the X and Y part.

Examples:

*Therapy*

If David is working with a client and he wants them to release an old behavior that doesn't serve them, he would first help them establish a new, positive behavior. Then he would simply say: "The faster your acknowledgment grows about the certainty to make these changes permanent (X), the stronger grows the forgetting of your memory of how to ever return to that old behavior (Y). Just forget about it. You're well established now, you have success (Outcome)." Those last two sentences are very simple. They are used to lock in the meaning of the sentence full of nominalizations.

*Selling A Window Frame*

"The more your conscious mind has that recognition of quality and sees that it is important (X), the more fluidly you'll find that you'll understand that this is really the proper window frame for this particular wall (Y). Just see it really clearly. It looks great (Outcome)."

EXERCISE: Write five nominalization patterns using the single bind. Then end each one with a simple statement, a command actually, of what you want the person to do.

---

**The human mind does not like confusion,
so it will latch on to any idea that makes sense.**

---

*Double Binds with Nominalizations*

As you may remember, double binds create the illusion of having two choices, each one offering a positive outcome. You might tell your kid (or husband): "You can take out the garbage before or after you clear the table." Either way, someone other than you is taking out the garbage.

Example:

"You can appreciate your ability to commit or you could simply gain comfort from the decisiveness of your mind's ability to see yourself already there."

EXERCISE: Write four double bind statements using nominalizations and end each one with a short, simple, direct statement of what you want them to do.

## PUNCTUATION AMBIGUITIES

These are tools that help deliver a message directly to the unconscious mind. As you use them, you will notice that people who are listening will easily overlook the strangeness of the sentences as if nothing were wrong.

To create a Punctuation Ambiguity, pick a word that can be used as both a noun and a verb or at least a word that has two different meanings.

This is your Pivot Word for the ambiguity. Once you have the pivot word, you work it into a sentence.

For example, the word *address* can mean the place where you live. It can also be what you do to an envelope. *Address* can also mean to speak to someone.

The punctuation ambiguity happens when the first part of a sentence seems to use the pivot word as a noun and what follows it makes it seem like a verb. This second part of the structure is phrased as a command.

Examples:

Address "...you might remember how you found your latest *address* me with more respect."

It sounds a little strange, but the conscious mind tends to overlook that because it doesn't fit into anything understandable. So it simply passes it by. This means the unconscious mind hears the command while the conscious mind does not.

Benefit "...and you can easily see, simply hear and convincingly feel how this can be of *benefit* by making a decision to do your homework now."

Block "...and you may be able to understand this in chunks so let me give you the first *block* out any hesitation about doing this."

Days "...and the beginning of that change may come about in hours or even *days* (*daze*) and confuse and eliminate any thoughts contrary to what I say."

Work "...you can find that things can be done a lot easier when you use this type of *work* this deeply into your mind."

Do you see how punctuation ambiguities work? Can you hear yourself saying them and feeling the benefits of using them?

By themselves, punctuation ambiguities will not persuade anyone to do something. But when you combine them with your other Power Persuasion techniques, they can give you profound influence.

Here are a few more Pivot Words. You can probably think of many more.

Debate
Fish
Fix
Flower
Fly
Force
Free
Glue
Happen
Heat
Home
Index
Land
Lead
Like
Loop
Love
Make
Map
Mark
Match
Microwave

Mind
Name
Open
Pay
Picture
Pile
Place
Power
Reveal
Ring
Seal
Salt
Shield
Shoot
Smoke
Tease
Tie
Toss
Understand
Veil
Write
X-ray

EXERCISE: Write at least five paragraphs that each have at least one punctuation ambiguity.

## PACING AND LEADING

This process allows you to give a series of commands or suggestions in a way that makes them easily accepted.

A Pace is anything that is true that cannot be argued. A Lead is something that is a suggestion or a command.

The easiest way to use this technique is to give several paces before you give a lead. To help you better understand how this flows, please read the following:

As the reader of this book, you've been reading the words, ideas and linguistic patterns and influence, and you've probably noticed that there are some very powerful patterns in this book. Some of these patterns are easily understood. Some, like "Fun with Nominalizations," might seem very advanced. All of the patterns in this book are very powerful. There's a lot of information in this book to incorporate. It's easy to see how using these patterns can increase your persuasive power. Take your time, be thorough in learning each one, and then incorporate it with all of the other patterns that you've learned.

Notice the flow of this statement, how it is interspersed with facts and commands. In this case facts can be described as truisms that cannot be argued. Commands are just that; they lead the flow of thought into a specific direction.

*The Pattern*

The most effective way to intersperse facts and commands is to do it in a gradual manner:

**Fact, Fact, Fact, Command**
**Fact, Fact, Command**
**Fact, Command**
**Command, Command, Command**

Now notice how this paragraph flows.

As the reader of this book (fact), you've been reading the words (fact), ideas and linguistic patterns, and influence (facts), and you've probably noticed that there are some very powerful patterns in this book (command). Some of these patterns are easily understood (fact). Some, like "Fun with Nominalizations," might seem very advanced (fact). All of the patterns in this book are very powerful (fact). There's a lot of information in this book to incorporate (fact). It's easy to see how using these patterns can increase your persuasive power (command). Take your time, be thorough in learning each one (command), and then incorporate it with all of the other patterns that you've learned (command).

Remember, a fact is *anything* that is true. *I am standing here, I am sitting here, you are talking, I am talking, you are listening, I am listening, the sky is blue* and *this room is yellow* are all facts.

There are two powerful ways to master pacing and leading: writing and speaking out loud. So be sure to do both exercises.

EXERCISE: Begin by knowing what your outcome is and writing it down. Then write three paragraphs interspersing facts and commands using the pattern of three facts followed by one command, two facts followed by one command, one fact followed by one command and finish with three commands.

EXERCISE: Try actually speaking this pattern spontaneously out loud, keeping in mind what a fact is. Use the pattern to intersperse facts with commands. Try doing this into a tape recorder and also with someone in front of you. It will put pressure on you to actually say something and keep the flow of conversation going.

## LOGICALLY SPEAKING

Remember default logic?

When someone says such things as *because, therefore, all of that leads to, that also causes*, or *justifies*, we tend to agree with what they are saying, even though it may not be true.

You can create "logical" sentences when you use these words as a sort of conjunction to join phrases and sentences.

Example:

"Being where you are and learning these language patterns is a lot similar to learning something that is very exciting *because* you know it's new and you know it's powerful and all of that is *justified* by the fact that you can influence people and cause them to create a great deal of enthusiasm and lead them in the direction that you want. You'll notice that in doing that *it logically helps* people come to just the right conclusion, which naturally is what you'll be looking for anyway, just because it makes sense."

Printed on the page, the above is quite long and ungainly. But when you're in a conversation with somebody and you have rapport with them, there are lots of things that they'll just sort of agree with.

Why?

Because.

## FUTURE PACING

This is one technique that you can use in almost any situation. You can always paint a picture that someone is going to see in the future.

Future Pacing is the process of taking your outcome and describing how someone would experience it in the future.

This is really important because you're not just explaining it to someone as she would have it now. You're also letting her experience it in her mind as already having had it for a while and feeling a sense of satisfaction or happiness, or whatever emotion you want to inject into it.

Examples:

*Selling High-End Windows*

Because buying windows and having them installed can be expensive, and there are so many factors to consider, prospects often stall on making a decision to buy. One of David's clients, who sold such windows, came up with:

"Mr. Smith, you've indicated the window which you think would best illuminate this portion of the room. Before you make any enjoyable decision on what you want, let me ask you to take a moment and imagine yourself next Spring with this window already installed. Take a look in your mind as you see how it would brighten up the room, and imagine what you'll see as you look outside and see your family playing on the other side. Notice what you say to yourself as they are laughing and having a fun time. As you get the feeling of that, go back to when you made that decision...now...do you like what you chose?"

He painted the picture in the future, which already distorted Mr. Smith from the present. Then he painted a wonderful picture of him looking out the window on a Spring day watching his family enjoying themselves and noticing the feelings he had. He went even further and had him remember back to right now to the decision he made and feeling good about it.

In doing that he made Mr. Smith go back and forth in time, which has a hypnotic effect. That's what makes this especially powerful.

EXERCISE: Practice this pattern. Ask someone to look to a time in the future, having made the decision and feeling good about it and remembering that decision now.

EXERCISE: Write three examples of future pacing, keeping your outcome in mind.

EXERCISE: This is the most important of these three exercises. Instead of writing or speaking, imagine learning and practicing all of the Power Persuasion skills in the future. See yourself practicing and feeling how you'll feel when you apply each of the techniques. Notice how the other person is responding. As you have that sense of confidence in your ability, look back on all the study and practice you did and how you can automatically use these techniques. It feels great, doesn't it?

Do this every day until you feel you have a good grasp of these skills.

## META MODEL LANGUAGE PATTERNS

These patterns seem harmless enough, but if you don't have rapport, they can easily be dissected and challenged. That's why rapport is so important when using these particular language patterns.

In addition to teaching you how to use Meta Model Language Patterns, we will also show you how to overcome them, something that is hard to do if you are in rapport with someone who is using them on you.

Before we introduce these patterns, please keep something in mind. Many of the patterns in this book get their names from technical NLP terms. It is not important to remember their names. What is important is how well you use them.

### Mind Reading

We've probably all done this or at least heard someone else do it.

Have you ever said: "I know what you're thinking" or "I know what you're probably thinking?" Well, that may or may not be true.

If you're on the receiving end of mind reading you could ask: "Well, how do you know? Is that really what I'm thinking or is it just what you're thinking that I'm thinking?"

Here we are, mind reading you:

You're obviously reading this book. You're thinking about how incredibly powerful it is to be able to apply every one of these patterns in your everyday life. As you're thinking about that, one of the things that can easily come to mind is that as you read this book, as you practice the techniques and you begin to review the power that each one of these language patterns has, it's easy to just begin to notice yourself thinking: "This stuff is truly powerful; this stuff has a great deal of energy to it."

That paragraph contains a great deal of mind reading. We just assumed what you are thinking and suggested it. Of course, people do this all the time in wrong ways.

If a crime has just been committed someone might say, "I'll bet you think I did it."

He is inadvertently placing that thought in someone's mind.

So be careful of your own mind reading. Make sure that you only suggest thoughts that you *want* people to have.

Examples:

*Selling A Car*

"Just being here, you probably want to smell the leather of these fine seats, don't you?"

*Stopping A Behavior*

"You're probably only doing this so you can get in trouble."

*Selling Clothing*

"Being here, you want to know what you might look like having a suit like that."

*Selling A House*

"You're probably thinking how nice it would be to own this house."

EXERCISE: Start making a list of all the things you want people to be thinking. Then practice them as mind reading patterns.

> ## In order for Meta Language Patterns to work, you must have rapport.

## LOST PERFORMATIVE

A Lost Performative is a statement that describes a judgment or belief or standard without describing the authority for saying it. Classic examples are: "It's the latest fashion" or "Everyone loves this."

Oh, really? Who says?

One typical way of using the lost performative in persuasion is along the lines of: "Decent people don't do that" or "This is the best suit for you."

Again, in order for such statements to be accepted, there has to be a great deal of rapport.

The lost performative is a favorite of politicians. You might hear one say something such as: "Welfare is the wasteful fat of society. We must cut it away to spare decent, honest people." Of course what he's not saying is: According to whom is it the fat of society?

The lost performative works particularly well when you provide three things that are true in front of it. Remember pacing?

Use the lost performative in a Pace, Pace, Pace, Lead structure.

For example, "You went to the store. You bought this book, you've taken the time to read this far, and you've got in your hands one of the most powerful instructional tools that you've ever purchased."

The lost performative is: "one of the most powerful instructional tools that you've ever purchased." Of course, we think it really is.

Examples:

*Selling Clothing*

"We carry the finest men's clothing in the state."

*Selling Financial Products*

"We offer the best financial advice you will ever find."

EXERCISE: Write down your outcome and create at least three lost performatives using the Pace, Pace, Pace, Lead format.

## CAUSE AND EFFECT

This is one of the most elegant and easiest-to-use language patterns, simply because it relies on our old friend, default logic. This pattern basically states that if you do X, Y will happen.

You use this pattern by just assuming that there is a cause and effect relationship between two things, though that is not necessarily the case.

Some of the more common cause and effect words and phrases are:

Because
Causes
Kindles
Creates
Leads to
Results in
Generates

Like all of the other patterns, this one relies on rapport. If you don't have rapport, some people will challenge what you say.

On the other hand, if you want to challenge someone else's cause and effect thinking, you would simply say: "Based on what? or "According to whom?"

Examples:

*Selling Clothing*

"Just being in this aisle, you'll see some styles you'll want to try on."

*Selling A House*

"The front door will remind you of home."

EXERCISE: Make a list of cause and effect words and start creating sentences you can use to influence someone. Begin to use this pattern in conversation. If you have rapport, nobody will notice.

## COMPLEX EQUIVALENT

This pattern always uses a form of the verb to be—*is, am, are.* It will sound something like: "It is a sin against God."

In making that statement, someone is equating whatever it is they are referring to and "sin against God" as being the same thing, which may or may not be true.

In another case, someone may say "Jim is a jerk." Being a friend of Jim, you could counter that by asking: "According to whom?"

Very few people know how to counter the complex equivalent, so this pattern has power.

Examples:

*Learning Power Persuasion*

"Understanding these language patterns is true knowledge."

*Selling Clothing*

"This suit is the best."

"This shirt is made for your shoulders."

At this point you may have noticed that people use Meta Model Language Patterns all the time. That is what makes them so deceptive and so powerful: they sound like everyday speech.

EXERCISE: Start combining this language pattern with others to see just how persuasive you can be.

## UNIVERSAL QUANTIFIERS

These are statements that imply or state absolute conditions as being true. They include such words as *always, never, everyone* and *everything*.

Someone using this pattern might say: "Everybody knows that's wrong" or "You never listen to me."

You can counter these statements by phrasing the universal quantifier in the form of a question. "Everybody?" "Never?" For effect, you might even punch the universal quantifier—"I NEVER listen to you?"

Examples:

*Stopping A Behavior*

"You'll never improve if you don't stop doing that."

*Selling Clothing*

"You'll always be in style wearing this."

"Everybody with good taste simply loves this dress."

*Convincing Someone to Try A New Restaurant*

"We always eat at those other places. Let's go to this new place."

## MODAL OPERATORS

These are words that suggest something that is necessary or possible to define the boundaries of someone's model of the world.

One example is, "If you want to live a good life, you must stop your sinful ways."

The modal operator in this example is *must.*

Other modal operators include:

Can (to describe an ability)
Have to
Got to
Need to
Can't

Modal operators can also demonstrate possibilities or capabilities.

A reality-type TV show presented a woman who was trying to overcome her fear of drowning by attempting to kayak down a stream. She was being coached by a man who said: "You must do it. You have to do it."

She replied, "I can't do it. I'm afraid."

He repeated with deep conviction, "You can do it. You must do it. You will do it."

And so she did.

So how can you apply this technique?

If someone is showing doubt about their ability to do something by saying they "can't do it," you could start by saying: "What if you could do it?"

Once you get agreement with *could*, you get them to agree that they *can*. At this point you're only talking about ability.

Next you add necessity. "You have to do it," you say.

You really can convince someone to commit an act they are afraid of or unwilling to do if you use a progression.

Be aware that modal operators can be used in unethical, even harmful ways.

Some unscrupulous police interrogators have been able to convince a suspect they knew was innocent to confess to a crime he did not commit.

They start out with something like: "We know you didn't do it, but could you do it? Not did you do it, but could you?"

Slowly, over the course of hours, they have the prisoner agree that he could do it.

Then the cops will start describing the opportunity and progress to greater agreements until they finally get a confession. The victim actually begins to think that he must have done it.

EXERCISE: With your outcome in mind, create at least five ways to use modal operators.

## UNSPECIFIED VERBS

Using Unspecified Verbs is a way to reach a conclusion about something without indicating how you arrived at that conclusion.

Someone might say: "You're going to be cast out of decent society."

You can counter this outrageous statement by asking: "Exactly how that will happen? What happens first? What is the next step?"

Unspecified verbs are used frequently in sales. The cover of a novel or DVD might promise that you will be entertained. But it doesn't say how you're going to be entertained.

Unspecified verbs can also describe your state of being or how you're going to be, without telling you how you're going to get there.

Examples:

*Selling A Car*

"Driving this car will make you feel like a king."

*Selling A Gym Membership*

"Working out here will give you that edge."

EXERCISE: Think of an outcome that you want. With that outcome in mind, start using each one of these Meta Model Language Patterns. Write them down and read them out loud. You may notice that they sound normal and flow easily. If not, adjust them until they do.

## DISTRACTED SENTENCING

This technique allows you to give a simple, easy suggestion or command during a moment of confusion.

To use Distracted Sentencing you insert a nonsense sentence or phrase (one out of context) in the middle of a group of other statements that would otherwise make perfect sense. Immediately follow the nonsense sentence with a suggestion or command, then continue with what you were saying before.

When selling a car, you might say something like: "This car has great acceleration yet it still has excellent gas mileage. The power train comes with a five-year warranty and the engine has 270 horsepower. *Dogs pulling bobsleds are trained completely by voice commands. Go ahead and get behind the wheel.* The seat has full lumbar support and can be adjusted automatically for each driver...."

Distracted sentencing also works well in a story.

For example, "My brother owns this car. He really loves it. He and his wife drove it across the country last year in five days and they never felt tired. *I wonder if people sleep better in small motels or big ones. Go ahead and get behind the wheel.*

My brother said the suspension was so solid that they never even noticed the bumps on some of those old country roads...."

This Power Persuasion technique works because the nonsense sentence causes the conscious mind to momentarily focus inward (going into a trance) trying to make sense of it, while the unconscious mind hears the suggestion or command.

The suggestion resolves the momentary confusion caused by the nonsense statement. Because people find confusion uncomfortable, they are likely to follow the suggestion because it offers a resolution.

The second way to use distracted sentencing is to occupy the conscious mind with words and ideas without context.

For example, out of the blue you might say: "My sister asked me if birds fly backwards in Australia." This is the perfect place for an imbedded command or reinforcing something that you know to be true for the listener.

A word of warning: Do not use distracted sentencing too often because it will create too much confusion. When people are confused, they don't buy.

EXERCISE: Practice this technique ALOUD, preferably speaking to another person, or into a tape recorder. This helps it enter the neurology of your brain and makes it more natural. You might start with a story about your day, for example, and interject a distracted sentence followed by a simple suggestion or command.

## HIDDEN DIRECTIVES (EMBEDDED COMMANDS)

These terms are used interchangeably.

This technique is so simple it may be hard to believe that it has so much power. But it really does.

To give you a sense of just how powerful it is, at one time, in order to learn it you had to pay a lot of money, and you had to be a psychologist, psychiatrist or a medical doctor.

Embedded Commands allow you to bypass the conscious mind so you can give direct suggestions and commands to the unconscious mind.

Hidden Directives fit into a sentence without calling attention to themselves.

You create them by marking out the commands with tonality, speed and pace.

Say the following sentence out loud:

It is possible to learn these language patterns and with repetition and practice gain some sense of mastery.

That's true, right? But nothing special.

Now say the sentence out loud and when you see...pause. Change your voice tone on the words in bold face. You might raise or lower it or go deeper. And say the bold face words just slightly slower than the rest of the sentence.

Ready?

Go.

It is possible to...**learn these language patterns**...and with repetition and...**practice**...**gain**...some sense of...**mastery**.

If you were to say that sentence to someone, her unconscious mind would hear: **"Learn these language patterns. Practice. Gain mastery."**

In order to get the best results with hidden directives, make sure you:

1. Determine your outcome.
2. Write it as a series of commands from one to four words long, such as, "buy my product."
3. Make the commands part of a normal sentence.
4. Mark these commands by pausing...and changing your voice.
5. Don't use just one hidden directive. Incorporate as many as you can into your proposal or pitch. The more embedded commands, the more persuasive you will be.

But what if someone catches me?

They won't. Strangers don't know your normal speaking style and people you already know might notice that you are doing something different, but they won't know what it is.

EXERCISE: Create an outcome and write short phrases that would work as embedded commands. With your outcome in mind, write at least one page on any subject, interspersing your embedded commands in the text. Make sure that it flows. Then read the page ALOUD.

## ERICKSONIAN HYPNOTIC PHRASING (a.k.a. WEASEL WORDS)

These phrases are based on the one of the techniques used by Milton Erickson, who was one of the foremost hypnotists of the last century. Erickson had a way of talking people into trance without giving any direct commands to close their eyes or relax. Instead, he would just sort of talk around the idea of going into trance and people would naturally do it.

These Ericksonian phrases are also known as Weasel Words because they allow you to weasel in a command without it being so direct or authoritarian.

For example, you might say to someone: "Consider why you want to do this." With some people, giving a command can create a great deal of resistance. A percentage of them just do not like to take orders so they won't respond to direct suggestion.

But what if you were to say: "I'm not entirely sure how well you can consider why you want to do this."

Here, you're not trying to force them to consider why. You're just asking them how well they might be able to consider why.

Now, in considering and interpreting that statement, the mind has to actually consider why they want to do this, to some degree.

When you use weasel words, the listener does not have something to object to.

In order to employ them you first determine your outcome.

In a hypnosis setting, one outcome would be for the client to relax.

Examples:

"A friend once NEVER told me, you know it's entirely possible to just get relaxed."

You're not telling the client to get relaxed. You're just repeating what a friend once said.

"After you come to a very comfortable conclusion that you can just relax, I'd like you to just notice something."

Again, you're not ordering them to relax, you're just saying that they can come to a conclusion.

"A person can completely relax."
You're just talking about people in general being able to relax.

There are hundreds of Ericksonian phrases that can be used for just about any outcome You can also create some of your own.

These phrases are very powerful, so please use them wisely.

EXERCISE: Write down an outcome. Then write out each of these phrases, or at least a couple dozen of them, followed by your outcome.

*Ericksonian Phrases*

A friend once NEVER told me to...
After you come to...
After you've...
And the more you X the more you Y
As a whole new way of thinking opens up...
All that really matters...
All that's really important...
Allowing yourself to just naturally...
Almost as if/though/like...
And (name) you know better than anyone that...
And as that occurs, you really can't help but notice...
And creating change like this...
And do you notice the beginning of...
And I think you're going to enjoy being surprised that...
And I want you to notice something that's happening to you...
And I wonder if you'll be curious as you notice...
And I wonder if you'll be curious about the fact that you...
And I'd like to have you discover...
And if you wish...
And it appears that already...
And it's very rewarding to know that...
And like magic...

And maybe you'll enjoy noticing...
And so it has been done...
And sooner or later, I don't know just when...
And that growing realization...
And that's just fine/all right/okay...
And the awareness that you've gained today...
And the genuine desire to really CHANGE once and for all...
And the ways in which you'll surprisingly use these learnings...
And then, now you'll discover...
And while you continue...
And while you wonder that, I want you to discover that...
And would you be willing to experience...
And you begin to wonder when...
And you can be pleased....
And you can really use it...
And you can wonder...
And you can wonder what...
And you will be surprised at...
And your unconscious mind can enable you to...
And, in an interesting way, you'll discover...
Another part of you that can take care of your comfort...
And that suggestion finds its mark...
At first..., but later...
At times like this some people enjoy...
Before you (name outcome), you can always simply (another or a
     related outcome)...
Can you notice...?
Continue by letting your unconscious...
Enable a particular resource to surface...
Even though you THINK it would have been hard...
Find that these changes positively in your future...
Give yourself the opportunity to see if...
Have you begun to notice that yet?
I want to remind you of something that you probably already know,
     which is...
I want you to enjoy this experience.
I wonder if you'd like to enjoy...
I wonder if you'll be interested, in learning how, to...

I wonder if you'll be pleased to notice...
I wonder if you'll be reminded...
I wonder if you'll be surprised to discover that...
I wonder if you'll decide to...or...
I wonder if you'll enjoy how naturally, how easily...
I wonder if you've noticed that...
I would like you to discover something...
I'd like you to begin allowing...
I'd like you to let yourself become more aware of...
In all probability...
If you could...
It is easy, isn't it...
It may be that you'll enjoy...
It may be that you're already aware of...
It's so nice to know...
It's going to be a pleasure to...
It's so easy, wasn't it...
It's very positive and comforting to know...
Keep changing your life just like this...
Kind of like...
Maybe it will surprise you to notice that...
Now I'd like you to have a new experience...
Now of course I don't know for sure what you're experiencing, but
    perhaps you're...
Obviously, naturally, convincingly, now...
One of the first things you can become aware of is...
One of the things I'd like you to discover is...
Perhaps beginning to notice...
Perhaps noticing...
Perhaps sooner than you expect...
Perhaps you wouldn't mind noticing...
Remember to forget to remember...
So just let it happen...
So now's the time...
So that it's almost as if...
That ongoing commitment to change...
The really important thing is to just be fully aware of...
The stuff reality is made of...

Very likely…
When would NOW be a good time…
With your permission…
You already know how to…
You don't need to be concerned if…
You'll be fascinated and feel a strong compulsion to…

# CHAPTER **10**

# Belief Changing Language Patterns

## OVERCOMING OBJECTIONS WITH SLEIGHT OF MOUTH

Sleight of Mouth patterns (SoM) are extremely short pithy comments, questions or responses that are designed to attack a belief or, in the case of sales, an objection.

If you pile enough of them on, you can absolutely destroy a belief.

This can be very dangerous. When you threaten strongly held beliefs, people become defensive. They may argue with you, especially if they feel humiliated, creating an uncomfortable situation.

So you must use SoMs with a great deal of grace, art and compassion.

## USING SLEIGHT OF MOUTH

The reason that SoMs are so effective is that they work on a higher level than the words that are spoken. They impact the very foundations of a belief.

### How To Recognize Beliefs

People state their beliefs in two ways.

The first is through Complex Equivalency, which basically is A = B. This might be stated as "Jim is a jerk," "This movie is great," "Chocolate is irresistible, " or "I'll never be able to master this."

These are simply beliefs, not facts. Facts are things that are indisputable: grass is green, this wall is painted blue.

Beliefs are also stated in terms of cause and effect. "Doing the books gives me an ulcer." "Talking to the boss makes me nervous." "Talking to beautiful women is scary."

Before learning the Sleight of Mouth patterns, keep something in mind. They are very simple, but very powerful.

Remember, people do not like having their beliefs challenged. So in addition to developing rapport, you're going to have to "soften" each of these patterns as you use them.

EXERCISE: Make a list of your beliefs, especially the ones that do not serve you. The latter are easy to determine. All you have to do is ask yourself what it is that is hard for you to do?

## SOFTENERS

Sleight of Mouth patterns can be harsh, abrasive and outright offensive. That is why it is critical to "soften" each of the SoMs when you use them.

By using softeners, you distance yourself from the confrontational aspects of an SoM and ease it into a more conversational framework.

Although there are many softeners, most fall into one of three categories.

### Quoting Others

"...John said that you are an inconsiderate fool...."

### Quoting Yourself

"...I'd wonder, if I were in your shoes...would I be an inconsiderate fool...."

### Presupposing Receptive Traits

"...you seem to be a person who wants it straight, and with that in mind, you're being an inconsiderate fool...."

Softeners can also be used in combination, in any order. If you wanted to use presupposing traits and quoting others, you might say: "Since you're a person of character and would want to hear the truth, John could say you're an inconsiderate fool."

## Some Other Softeners Are:

"I had a brother who used to believe (insert belief) and then he realized (SoM)"
"This may sound silly but (SoM)"
"I am curious as to (SoM)"
"Let me ask you (SoM)"
"I'm just wondering... (SoM)"

EXERCISE: Write three strong statements or outright insults using each of the three primary softeners.

## SLEIGHT OF MOUTH PATTERNS

We have left out softeners in the following examples in order to simplify the process. However, please be sure to use them in real life.

## ATTACKING THE SOURCE OF A BELIEF

As its name implies, this pattern questions the origin of a belief. Some typical phrases are:

"Where did you get that from?"
"What could cause you to make that decision?"
"According to whom?"
"Have you checked the source?"
"How did you reach that conclusion?"
"Who told you to think that?"
"Well, it's possible that's based on faulty logic, isn't it?"

Here are some beliefs with examples of this SoM pattern.

Belief: "Jim is a jerk."

SoM: "Where did you get *that* from?"

Belief: "It's hard for me to talk to women"

SoM: "Did someone tell you to believe that or did you come up with it all on your own?"

Belief: "It's hard to close a sale."

SoM: "According to *whom?*"

Belief: "Don't talk to him. He's a loser."

SoM: "Really? How'd you come up with that crazy idea?"

EXERCISE: Look at your list of beliefs that don't serve you and use this technique to destroy those negative beliefs. If you believe that cold calling is hard, ask yourself: "According to whom?" "Where did I get that from?" Every time that you challenge a belief using a Sleight of Mouth pattern you're going to have to go inside and internally review it, which steps you away from the actual belief.

Do this repeatedly, four and five times. It gives you a different perspective. This is what you're going to be doing when you use these SoM patterns on someone.

EXERCISE: Write at least five examples of this type of SoM with softeners.

**THE META FRAME**

You use the Meta Frame to attack the belief directly.

Belief: "Jim is a jerk."

SoM: "How is it possible to believe that Jim is a jerk?"

"How could you believe that Jim is a jerk?"

Belief: "I need to wait."

SoM: "How is it possible that the future is going to be easier than the past? Because, as a person who knows that opportunities can be fleeting, isn't waiting the thing you need to avoid?"

Belief: "I will have to talk to my boss."

SoM: "Could it be that you haven't yet considered the amount of decision-making ability your boss has already bestowed on you?"

Let's look at some of the limiting beliefs you may have and how to change them.

Belief: "It's difficult to close a sale."

SoM: "How is it possible to believe that? Take a look at that. How *is it* possible?"

Belief: "It's difficult to talk to women."

SoM: "How can you believe that? They make up half the population."

EXERCISE: Write at least four examples of the meta frame. Be sure to include softeners.

EXERCISE: Use the meta frame on your own limiting beliefs.

## USING THE CRITERIA AGAINST ITSELF

Remember that one way that beliefs are stated linguistically is A = B.

If someone says "Jim is a jerk, *Jim* is A and *is a jerk* is B.

To change the belief, you can use A or B against itself.

Belief: "Jim is a jerk."

SoM: "Jim is a jerk? Only a jerk would say something like that."

Belief: "John is a good guy."

SoM: "You're too good a guy to believe that."

Belief: "You're not my type."

SoM: "You're not really the type to have types, are you?"

When someone makes a cause and effect statement (A causes B), you can apply either the cause (A) or the effect (B) against itself.

Belief: "Listening to you makes me crazy."

SoM: "Listening to me only causes you to hear my words." (applying the cause against itself)

Belief: "If I buy this I will go broke."

SoM: "How can you buy what you just said?" (applying the cause against itself)

"You'll go broke thinking like that." (applying the effect against itself)

Apply this technique to your own beliefs.

Belief: "Cold calling is hard."

SoM: "No, it's hard to believe that it's hard."

"No, cold calling is just picking up the phone."

Belief: "It's difficult to talk to women."

SoM: "No, it's difficult to talk with your mouth full of food."

"Well, you're not in the type of social situations where you're forbidden to speak, are you?"

EXERCISE: Write at least four examples of this SoM and include any softening phrases.

## FOCUSING ON THE INTENT OF THE BELIEF

Many of the things we do and believe are self-destructive. The reason we don't change is that we get a secondary benefit from these actions and beliefs.

If you find yourself unable to lose weight, for example, it may be that having a larger body makes you feel less vulnerable in what you may perceive as a dangerous world. Or, being heavy may be a way of avoiding sexual encounters.

With this technique, you are trying to determine what the benefit of having a certain belief is, or you can simply imply a motive for the belief.

Belief: "I need more time to think about it."

SoM: "Are you really trying to buy more time? What sort of benefit could you get from waiting?"

Belief: "I'm not pretty."

SoM: "Well, I'm really trying to figure out what sort of outcome you would have by believing that you're not pretty. Is it that you're looking for attention, or do you just want to sound like everyone else because you think that's what you're supposed to say?"

By now you've probably found that using these Sleight of Mouth techniques on your own beliefs has loosened them up considerably.

You are using them on your own beliefs—right?

If not, please use them to start creating a happier, more powerful you.

EXERCISE: Review your list of limiting beliefs and apply the SoM techniques to them.

EXERCISE: Create a list of beliefs held by people you want to influence. If you're in sales, list the common objections you get. You can use this technique before the objection actually comes up (more on this later).

## ATTACKING THE METHODOLOGY OF THE BELIEF

SoM patterns can be very abrasive, so be sure to have rapport when doing this technique. Also, soften the SoM by asking a sincere question, or softening your tone of voice.

Belief: "I could never vote (Democrat/Republican)."

SoM: "Never? Have you ever asked yourself just how you came to that belief, because there are a lot of things that you haven't thought about. Maybe it's only because your parents are (Democrat/Republican)."

Belief: "There is no way I could consider you as anything but a friend."

SoM: "Hmmm…I'm trying to understand…just how you came to that decision because there are so many paths to arrive at a decision. What else are you not thinking about?"

Their answer is not important. What is important is that they are willing to reconsider the methodology they used to reach their decision.

EXERCISE: Write at least five examples of this type of SoM, including softeners.

## CHANGING THE FRAME SIZE

You change the Frame Size of a belief by Chunking Up, Chunking Down or Chunking Laterally.

## CHUNKING UP TO A HIGHER VALUE

You chunk up by asking a question about a larger belief or structure that controls that particular belief.

When someone states a belief you might ask such questions as:

"What is the purpose of that?"
"That's an example of what?"
"What's important about this/that?"

Anytime you ask this type of question it implies that there is something bigger beyond the belief. When they answer, you use that response against the original belief.

Belief: "I have to talk to the wife/boss before I buy this."

SoM: "What's important about that?"

Answer: "I want his/her respect."

SoM: "And when a good decision like this purchase is completed that respect will be reciprocated. Won't it?"

Belief: "I have to win this contest."

"SoM: "What's important about winning this contest?"

Answer: "It will prove that I'm good enough."

SoM: "You're good enough whether you win or not."

Belief: "I really wouldn't take part in a business like that."

SoM: "Is that the example of someone critically looking at their outcome or is that the example of a snap decision?"

EXERCISE: Write at least four examples of chunking up, including softeners.

## CHUNKING DOWN

You can chunk down by using universal qualifiers.

Belief: "Computers are useless."

SoM: "For everyone?"

Belief: "I can't afford it."

SoM: "Ever?"

Belief: "There are no good shows on TV."

SoM: "Never?"

You can also chunk down a portion of a belief that the person has not yet noticed.

Belief: "I don't have time to study."

SoM: "Do you have time to make money? Because studying is about learning how to apply knowledge to business."

Belief: "I don't want to go out."

SoM: "Do you like coffee and talking with friends?"

Answer: "Yes."

SoM: "Well, instead of going out let's have coffee and talk. Besides that is what we would do anyway."

EXERCISE: Write at least four examples of this SoM, including softeners.

EXERCISE: Go out into the world and apply the SoMs you've learned so far.

---

**When using SoMs, it is critical to maintain rapport.**

---

## CHUNKING LATERALLY

In order to chunk laterally you have to ask yourself: "What is this exactly like?" or "What is this similar to?"

Belief: "I can't buy this suit."

SoM: "Yeah, but you can buy *this* suit (showing them another one)."

Belief: "I'm too old to learn how to fly an airplane."

SoM: "Are you too old to learn to drive a car?"

Belief: "It's hard for me to lose weight."

SoM: "What if you went and lost the weight anyway, but you let it be hard?"

Belief: "I can't go forward with my life until I get out of this relationship."

SoM: "What if you changed and stayed in the relationship anyway?"

EXERCISE: Write four examples of this SoM, using softeners.

> **Some of the SoMs make absolutely no sense;**
> **their power lies in the delivery.**

## THE REDEFINE

When someone believes that A = B or that A causes B, you tell them that in reality, A = C or A causes C.

Belief: "Learning Power Persuasion causes you to care more about results than people." (A causes B)

SoM: "It is not that it causes you to care less about people. It causes you to care enough to give people the reasons they want to be happy with their decisions."

Belief: "Your product is too expensive." (A = B)

SoM: "It is not that it is expensive. This one is of exceptional quality."

Belief: "You're not my type." (A = B)

SoM: "It's not that I'm not your type. It's that you know you want to be treated special…in a way that you really like…and you want to know that you can feel that…with me."

EXERCISE: Write at least four examples of the redefine, including softeners.

## METAPHOR

When you use a metaphor, you are basically creating a story. One of the ways you can do this is similar to chunking laterally. You ask yourself, "What is this like?" but in terms of something that is slightly different.

For example, if someone asks what it is like to lose weight, a good metaphor might be: "walking up a hill with a heavy backpack and discarding things out of it along the way."

Belief: "I don't think I can do that."

SoM: "The Bible says that if you have the faith of a mustard seed you can move a mountain. So I ask you, is your faith at least as big as a mustard seed?"

You can also cite or quote someone who is close to you or someone from history.

Belief: "I can't spend the time I would like to with your group."

SoM: "You know, my brother has a family and a fulltime job, just like you. When I told him the real need we have for help here, he knew he had to help and he made time to...*put in the time*...and I know just how important time is to him." Notice the imbedded suggestion.

EXERCISE: Choose four outcomes and write a metaphor for each.

## CONSEQUENCES

This SoM pattern relies on pointing out the end result of a belief.

When someone tells you a belief, think about its painful consequences and then communicate them.

Belief: "I am too old to learn how to fly."

SoM: "Do you realize that in that one sentence, you just talked yourself out of a wonderful life of flying, of learning new skills and experiencing new adventures in the air?"

Belief: "I don't think I'm attractive."

SoM: "Do you realize that as long as you hold that belief, you are denying good feelings about yourself?"

Belief: "I can't buy that."

SoM: "Stop for just a moment and really think to yourself how believing that you can't is going to affect you very deeply. Do you want that?"

EXERCISE: Write at least four consequences for beliefs that people have. Be sure to do this on your own beliefs, as well.

## REALITY

With this SoM you are basically asking someone how they know that a belief is true.

Belief: "I don't want to go to therapy."

SoM: "How do you determine which problems only you can solve and those for which you must ask help?"

Belief: "All of this is too much for me to learn."

SoM: "How do you know that? At your age you've learned a lot already. Are you saying you're going to stop learning?"

Belief: "It's not right to give money to panhandlers."

SoM: "What is the real test between a panhandler and a man asking for a church donation?"

EXERCISE: Write at least four examples of this SoM and include any softeners.

## COUNTER EXAMPLE

You introduce an example that is contrary to someone's stated belief.

Belief: "I hate this ugly coat."

SoM: "You're going to love it when it's 30 below zero."

Another way to do this technique is to chunk down. Do they ALWAYS believe something is true? Has there ever been a time when A does not equal B?

Then give a counter example.

Belief: "Murder is absolutely wrong."

SoM: "If you knew that killing a madman was the only way to prevent the death of a family member, would it be wrong to murder that man?"

Belief: "I can't get this job done in that amount of time."

SoM: "If you knew that your income, paying your mortgage, and the happiness of your family all depended on you doing the job in that amount of time, could you do it?"

Belief: "I'm too old to learn something new."

SoM: "You learned how to cash your Social Security check, didn't you?"

EXERCISE: Write at least four examples, using softeners. Start applying them to the people around you and to yourself.

## ANOTHER OUTCOME

This SoM pattern most resembles sleight-of-hand, where the magician distracts you from a clandestine movement he is making.

When you use this technique, you are distracting someone from their original outcome to another one.

For example, you might say: "Whether X is true isn't really the issue, but rather…"

Or "It's not that X is really the issue, but rather…"

Belief: "It's too expensive."

SoM: "Whether it's too expensive or not isn't really the issue, but rather that you are satisfied on into the future with the purchase of this product."

Belief: "There's no way that I would visit THAT city. The crime rate is too high."

SoM: "As I see it, it's not really that the crime rate is high, because millions of people live there without trouble. It's that the city is so different from what you know that makes it scary."

Belief: (teenager) "I own a car. Why won't you let me go out? You're trying to control me."

SoM: (parent) "It really isn't about control; it's about safety. It's about how much I care and about how much I love you."

EXERCISE: Write at least four examples of this technique, using softeners.

> **In order to change beliefs with SoMs, you must use several of them.**

## THE THRESHOLD

With this pattern you are extending the belief to its ultimate negative or ridiculous conclusion.

Belief: "I don't think I can quit smoking."

SoM: "Are you willing to hold on to that belief until you're dead?"

Belief: "It's hard to do cold calls."

SoM: "Do you know how ultimately that belief will hold you back and make you poor for the rest of your life?"

Belief: "It's hard to talk to people I don't know."

SoM: "Do you realize that if you keep that belief, you will be alone the rest of your life?"

Belief: "I need to think about it for a while."

SoM: "If I gave you a year, could you make a decision by that time? What do you think you would have already decided by then?"

EXERCISE: Write at least four examples, using softeners.

## APPEALING TO A HIGHER CRITERIA

To use this SoM pattern, you first ask questions to learn the criteria behind someone's belief.

Two of the most useful questions are: "What is that an example of?" and "What is important about that?"

Belief: "This is too hard for me to learn."

SoM: "What is that an example of?"

Answer: "My previous experience."

SoM: "Well, in your past experience, haven't there been times when you've learned things?"

Belief: "I won't pay any more than X for this."

SoM: "What's important about that?"

Answer: "Getting the best value."

SoM: "Can you see that what you really are buying is value, not price?"

Belief: "I have to talk to my boss."

SoM: "What's important about that?"

Answer: "I want to show respect for my boss."

SoM: "When you make the right decision, don't you get respect from people who are above you?"

EXERCISE: Write at least four examples, with softeners.

## MODEL OF THE WORLD (SWITCHING REFERENTIAL INDEX)

This pattern requires that you ask someone if their belief is true for everyone's model of the world, or if their model of the world has always held true.

As we teach you this pattern, we also want to show you how you can start combining Sleight of Mouth patterns.

Belief: "If this is so good, why haven't I heard of it before?"

SoM: (Model of the World) "Is it always true that you must have heard about something in order for it to be good?" Here you might want to add a metaphor. "Electricity was around for millions of years before anybody heard about it. Does that mean it wasn't good until they heard about it?"

Belief: "It's too expensive."

SoM: (Model of the World) "It's true that a lot of people do confuse value with expense." Now you could switch to Using Criteria Against Itself. "That's a pretty expensive belief to have, don't you think? That could be a very costly belief in the long run."

EXERCISE: Write at least four examples, using softeners.

## REVERSING PRESUPPOSITIONS

You can use this technique to help someone realize that the opposite of what they believe can be both true and helpful.

Basically, you're asking: "How does the opposite of your belief actually cause a better outcome?"

It follows this pattern:

|  | (is, does) | (cause) | |
|---|---|---|---|
| **How** | (has, would) | **opposite of your belief** (make) | **more of your outcome?** |
|  | (can, could) | (mean) | |
|  | (might) | (equal) | |

Belief: "It's too expensive."

SoM: "If you believed that it was the right price at what it costs, could you see how you could easily get it and start enjoying the benefits?"

Belief: "I am too old to learn this."

SoM: "How could being the age you are right now be exactly the right time for you to start learning?"

Belief: "It's too hard to stop smoking."

SoM: "Could you see how believing that it's easy to quit smoking would give you what you want sooner?"

Let's stack on a couple more SoMs on this pattern to really shake the foundations of a limiting belief.

Belief: "I am not creative."

SoM: (Attacking the Origin of the Belief) "Who ever told you that you're not creative? Every day you have to be creative in order to live. (Threshold) Can you see how that belief alone is going to hold you back? (Reversing Suppositions) Can you see how believing that you do have artistic skills is going to give you a lot more creative resources?"

EXERCISE: Write at least four examples of reversing suppositions, with softeners.

EXERCISE: Add at least one more SoM to each of your examples.

## EXAMINING IDENTITY

When you use this technique, you are attacking the identity of the person who holds the belief.

This pattern can be very direct and powerful, so it requires a great degree of sensitivity and compassion, as well as skillful use of softeners.

Belief: "This is too hard. I don't want to do it."

SoM: "Do you want to be the kind of person who gives up on things that are important? Is that how you want people to see you?"

If you choose, you can use this pattern to be direct and sarcastic.

Belief: "You're not my type."

SoM: "Oh, you're the type of person who has types." Notice that this response also employs using criteria against itself.

Now, let's stack up the SoMs.

Belief: "You're not my type."

SoM: (Using Criteria Against Itself) "Oh, you're the type of person who has types. (Counter Example) It's not that you're looking for a type; it's that you're looking for a feeling that a type would give you. (Methodology of Belief) How did you reach the conclusion that a certain type of person is the one who's going to make you happy?"

## COMBINING SoMs TO CHANGE INDIVIDUAL BELIEFS

Here's where you really learn to pile on the SoMs.

Let's say someone you care for believes that it's hard to quit smoking.

(Attacking the Source of the Belief) "Do you believe it's hard to quit smoking because of your experience or because you just haven't thought of any other excuse? (Meta Frame) In the cooking business we call that belief a crock. Think of how many people have quit smoking. Millions have. (Using Criteria Against Itself) It's not hard to quit smoking; it's hard to die of lung cancer. (Focusing on the Intent of the Belief) What possible benefit could you get from believing that? Just by thinking that it's hard, you're going to make it difficult for yourself. (Attacking the Methodology of the Belief) How could you possibly come to a conclusion like that? Are you doing it just out of ignorance? (Chunking Up) What's important about believing that stopping smoking is hard?" (Answer) "I don't want to hurt." (Response) "Can you imagine how much it's going to hurt dying of emphysema? Can you imagine how much it's going to hurt your family?"

If you really want to hammer somebody's belief about quitting smoking, here's how you can use more of the Sleight of Mouth patterns.

(Chunking Down) "In what way specifically is it hard to quit smoking?" Or, "Is it always hard to quit smoking?"

(Chunking Laterally) "Why don't you quit smoking and make it hard anyway? You'd get what you want, wouldn't you?"

(Redefine) "No, it's not hard to quit smoking. It's easy to quit smoking. It's hard to die of lung cancer."

(Metaphor) "It's hard to quit smoking? Well, I knew a person who used to believe it was hard until that one time she looked in her grandchildren's eyes and realized how much she loved them and how important it was for them; and in that moment, she decided it didn't matter how hard it was. She decided to quit."

(Consequences) "Think of that belief for a moment, if you would. If you hold on to that belief, do you know how hard it's going to be to ever quit? Do you know how much that belief alone is going to hold you back?"

(Reality) "How do you know it's hard to quit smoking? Have you done it in every possible circumstance?"

(Counter Example) "Would you believe that it's hard to quit smoking if a doctor told you that you couldn't get near your daughter's oxygen tent with a cigarette?"

(Another Outcome) "Whether it's hard or not to quit smoking is not really the issue. The issue is, is it important for you to quit smoking?"

(Threshold) "If you believe it's hard to quit smoking, can you imagine how your life is going to suffer as you continue to believe that? It's not worth it."

(Appealing to a Higher Criteria) "What's important to you?"

It could be family, love, peace of mind or some spiritual values. Once you know, all you have to say is: "If you believe stopping smoking is difficult, do you realize that it will never give you the peace of mind or the love that you really really want? Because that's what you want, isn't it?"

(Model of the World) "Do you really think that everyone has a hard time quitting smoking? Because they don't. They just quit."

(Reversing Presuppositions) "How would believing that it's easy actually make it simpler to quit smoking?"

(Identity) "Come on, do you really want to be the type of person who's going to believe that they don't have control of their life? Because you're not that type of person."

Note: At first glance, chunking up and appealing to a higher criteria can appear to be the same thing, but there is a subtle difference.

Chunking up is asking yourself: "What is this an example of that is bigger?" For example, a beautiful woman not going out with you is an example of how some people turn their backs on great opportunities.

Appealing to a higher criteria is a form of chunking up, but it is much more personal to the person you are persuading. Using the same example, you might find out that her not going out with you might be because it seems too risky for her, and she values her security.

Security is her higher value that you would want to appeal to.

In using BOTH chunking up and appealing to higher criteria you might say: "I understand your hesitation. I have a great and wise friend who once took me by the hand (take her hand) and looked right into my eyes and said (insert softener) "you're right." You don't TRULY know the type of opportunity you're walking away from until you're absolutely certain that you can feel safe, secure, and only then...give yourself permission...(imbedded suggestion) to enjoy it."

EXERCISE: Pick some of your limiting beliefs and apply every one of the SoMs to them. Be sure to do this. You don't want to be the type of person who doesn't do the things that will make your life better, do you?

## MORE SLEIGHT OF MOUTH EXERCISES

You can use SoM patterns before an objection occurs to inoculate against it. When you add softeners, SoMs can be very effective.

For example, if you anticipate that somebody will object to the price of your offering, you might say beforehand: "...and when it comes to its cost of $1,000, I used to get people telling me it's too expensive (quoting someone else). But I don't know what changed. Maybe they realized it was too expensive NOT to buy it, or they actually began looking at HOW they figured whether or not something was expensive."

EXERCISE: Write the five most common objections you encounter then write at least three SoMs that would inoculate against them.

EXERCISE: Create a debate with yourself in which you play both sides and respond only with SoMs.

EXERCISE: Engage in a Sleight of Mouth battle with a partner. Make sure that both of you do this in a humorous, amiable way, despite being in an "argument."

> **Piling on SoMs can destroy a belief.**
> **Do this with caution.**

# CHAPTER 11

# Some Final Thoughts

Congratulations! You've finished reading Power Persuasion.

Now go back and read it again.

The more you study and practice these techniques, the more effective you will become at influencing your loved ones, friends, business associates and others whose cooperation you need for any worthy purpose.

As you learn and apply these skills, you will gain a greater understanding of how the human mind works, including your own.

This knowledge is priceless.

You can use what you learn here to change your life in dramatic ways. You can also use your new-found power to encourage the people you care about to believe in themselves and look for positive solutions to their challenges.

We strongly encourage you to use this power in an ethical manner, and hopefully, with wisdom. You do not have the right to control or manipulate others, or make life-changing decisions for them.

But sometimes, when you see someone you care about foundering and looking for help, it may be appropriate to use your persuasion ability to help free them from limiting beliefs.

NEVER use Power Persuasion to harm another. Use it only to benefit all concerned.

Remember that there is no single most-powerful language pattern.

And none of them will work without rapport. Make sure that establishing rapport is your first outcome.

And you can't have rapport if you're only thinking about what you're going to say next; this is why you must practice these techniques until they become automatic.

All of the Power Persuasion techniques require you to really pay attention to the people you are attempting to influence, and most importantly, the people you are trying to help.

You have to feel like them, as if you're willing, just for a moment, to get inside their skin and be who they are, so that you can pay attention and guide them in the direction that you want them to go.

So really work on developing rapport by listening, reflecting back what people are saying, and letting your body move in the same way their body moves.

If you do none of the other techniques, you will still have tremendous influence.

# Biographies

David R. Barron is a communication and persuasion expert trained in Hypnosis, Neuro-Linguistic Programming and Social Influence. Since 1999 he has worked as a clinical hypnotist with his company Changeworks Hypnosis, with over 3000 hours of one-on-one work with clients. He has also worked as a corporate consultant and seminar trainer, leading workshops on persuasion and self-improvement.

For over two years Barron consulted with InnVision, a leader in helping the homeless and disadvantaged find greater resources within themselves to feel more empowered. He has appeared on hundreds of radio and TV shows and has contributed to such magazines as Advance and Maxim.

Mr. Barron can be reached at dr.barron@changework.com and you can see his web site at www.power-persuasion.com.

Danek S. Kaus has written hundreds of articles on business and personal development for dozens of business and general interest publications.

He is a former clinical hypnotist who has trained doctors and nurses in hypnotic medical techniques. In his work as an independent publicist and consultant, he has helped clients obtain free media exposure in literally thousands of TV and radio shows, newspapers and magazines.

Mr. Kaus can be reached at dkaus@sbcglobal.net